The

A

S

reting

L

Kim Hungerford

Hayden-McNeil Publishing Inc.

· Printed in the United States of America

10 9 8 7 6 5 4 3 2 1

ISBN 1-57182-326-3

Hayden-McNeil Publishing
47461 Clipper
Plymouth, Michigan 48170
(313) 455-7900

For information regarding a video of the material presented on
the CD-ROM, please contact Hayden-McNeil Publishing at the
number listed above.

ACKNOWLEDGEMENTS

First and foremost I would like to thank Richard Ellis, without whose mastery of ASL and interpreting this product would never have become a reality. My appreciation for his input and patience throughout this project can never be fully expressed. I would also like to thank Bill and Janet Schwall as the models for the accompanying CD-ROM whose language skills made this project complete. And finally, I would like to thank the amazingly talented staff at Hayden-McNeil Publishing, Inc. for their skills and professionalism in the development and production of this work.

BIOGRAPHIES

Bennett B. Borden is the owner and Executive Director of Sign Language Consultants, a training and consulting firm in Washington, D.C. Mr. Borden has been an interpreter for more than ten years and is nationally certified. Mr. Borden worked in a variety of positions including Staff Interpreter for the Central Intelligence Agency and as the Virginia Quality Assurance Screening Coordinator before beginning his own company. He currently lives in the Washington, D.C., metropolitan area where he continues to develop training materials for ASL interpreters.

As a native ASL user, Janet Etkie Schwall comes from a Deaf family and has been an ASL instructor for various colleges. She currently works at Madonna University as a Sign Language Studies Instructor in Michigan. Janet, a 1991 graduate of Gallaudet University, is the director of Deaf Youth Leadership at Deaf Community Advocacy Network. Janet is serving as board member on several boards.

"Learning American Sign Language is rewarding because it is a three-dimensional language with a unique structure and order. ASL is a very precious part of the Deaf community." - Janet Etkie Schwall

Billy Schwall is a native ASL user and comes from a Deaf family. He currently works for the Michigan Relay Center as a Service Assistant where he translates ASL gloss into conversational English and vice versa on relay calls. In addition to his duties at Ameritech, he teaches Deaf culture, ASL, and the functions of Telecommunication Relay Services. Billy is one of the founders of The Deaf Michigander newspaper in 1992 and the Deaf Nation newspaper in 1995. He attended Gallaudet University for three years and holds a B.A. degree from Spring Arbor College.

"We are now in the midst of an ASL revolution where ASL is beginning to be recognized and accepted by many. Let this book/CD-ROM be one of many resources available to our society." - Billy Schwall

The Art of Interpreting

CHAPTERS

Language: Use and Development

Let us begin our discussion of American Sign Language (ASL) with a look at language in general. Go back with me, if you will, to the earliest beginnings of language and imagine how a particular language developed. Each of us experiences things in our world. We see objects, we have feelings, and we make relationships between all of these things and form thoughts. Humans are social creatures and are driven by a need to communicate the things we experience. When we encounter another person, we want to be able to share these thoughts in our minds with them. The essence of language is this need to communicate.

Communication develops in a very standard way. When we are alone, we experience things in the world (a tree, the sky, a bird) and we have no need to label them. We have but to understand them and to be able to call up the picture of them in our minds later.

Now put two of us together. We are both looking at one object, a tree, for example. I have a picture of this tree in my mind, which has been recorded there through my experience. Because we have no name for it, the only way to communicate this to you would be for me to actually bring you to the tree and point to it, or possibly draw a picture of it. This is how languages developed originally, with a graphic representation of objects in the real world.

However, there is a limit to the effectiveness of this. Suppose I have seen or experienced something that you have not. If you have never experienced a tree in any way, then my representation of that tree will mean nothing to you. Therefore, no communication can occur. Granted, I could still bring you to the object and let you experience it, but this is certainly a cumbersome way to communicate.

Secondly, we cannot communicate about anything that does not have a tangible reference in the real world. How would I describe a feeling of love, hate, or anger? What about ideas and concepts such as freedom, loyalty, and independence? These cannot be represented by a picture. Therefore, a new way to communicate has to be developed. Let's go back to our example of a tree. You and I both know what a tree is, and we both have a picture

1

of it stored in our memories. We are both inside a house, and I think of a tree and want to communicate this to you. I draw a picture of a tree, and it causes the concept you have stored in your mind to come into your mental view. Thus, we both are now imagining the same, or similar things. I have caused a mental image to appear in your mind. You and I decide to name this thing so that we can speak about it. We decide to call it tree. Now every time I want this picture to come into your mind, I simply have to speak the name we have agreed upon, and it causes the image to appear. This is communication.

Using this very simple example, we can understand how all systems of communication developed. A group of individuals experiencing similar things in the real world eventually develop a system of names for the objects, thoughts, actions, and emotions they observe and experience. The more they interact, the more complex the systems become. Systems of how to put words together are created and agreed upon, and full languages eventually appear. However, we must never forget that all of these grand systems of grammatical rules develop from a very basic process of labeling objects, feelings, and ideas in the real world. Thus all languages are conceptual in nature.

All of this was put together in a theory by a man named Charles Peirce (pronounced purse) in the 1800s. He said that for communication to occur there are three things that must exist.

1   Object:

This is the item in the real world which is being discussed: a tree, a bird, or love. It is the actual occurrence in the real world which we represent by a name or phrase.

2   Representamen:

This is the name which we give the object. The letters placed in the order T-R-E-E represent the tall leafy object out in the real world.

3 Interpretant

This is the mental image that links the representamen with the object. In other words, when we see or hear the word tree, it has to trigger a memory in our minds which brings up a picture of a tree. If the word we see or hear has no representation in our minds, there is no communication.

This theory that Mr. Peirce developed really makes sense. If I say the word tree, you must recognize that word, you must have learned it somewhere and linked it to the actual object in the real world, and then it must cause the image of the actual tree to come into your mind for communication to occur. If any of the three pieces are missing, we cannot communicate. If I say the word "equi" to you, only those who have this representamen, or name, in their minds, and who have linked it to an object in the real world will gain any understanding. "Equi" is the Latin word for horses.

We now understand how basic communication works. I say a word; you have learned it and linked it to a real object, feeling, or idea; and it causes this object, feeling, or idea to be reproduced in your mind so that you and I understand each other.

Basic Communication

Let's throw in a little twist to the situation. Suppose you and I have grown up learning separate systems of communication, meaning we speak different languages. You and I want to communicate. Now, we could go back to the old way of gesturing to the specific object and go through all that, but then we would be ignoring hundreds of years of advancement. So we need a third party to interpret between us.

In my mind, I have a picture of an exact object that I want to communicate to you. I have no access to your list of representamen that will cause the correct interpretant to appear in your mind. Meaning, I don't know which particular word from your vocabulary to utter to cause the picture I have in my mind to appear in yours. I say the word I know and have linked to the object, "книга", but it has no effect. When we add the interpreter, we can communicate if certain things are true. Let's look at what the interpreter must have in his mind in order to do his job well.

Role of the Interpreter:

The interpreter must have a familiarity with both lists of representamen, meaning he has to know both languages. But more importantly, he has to know how the two relate to each other. He has to have, in effect, two different representamen linked to the same object in his mind. Using our earlier example of the Latin word "equi", if he were interpreting between an English speaker and a person fluent in Latin, he would have both of these words, "equi" and "horses", linked to the real-world object of the four-legged-pretty-running-things in his mind. If he didn't have them correctly linked, miscommunication would occur. For example, if instead of having the word "equi" linked to horses, he had it linked to rabbits, miscommunication would occur.

Now assume our interpreter has both sets of representamen, or languages, and has them linked to the right objects. I say the word "КНЙГА", and it causes a mental picture of the object I am thinking of to appear in the mind of the interpreter. This is the first, most crucial step. If the interpreter doesn't understand and get the right image in his mind, then the process fails from the start. So now all we have to do is get the picture from the interpreter's mind into yours. The interpreter looks for the English representamen, or word, that is linked to that object in the real world and speaks it to you, "book". Now the word he speaks triggers an interpretant to appear in your mind, and a mental picture of a book is produced.

This is what we must remember when signing or interpreting; we are communicating concepts, not words. Therefore, we must not look to words as the source of our interpretation, but the mental image those words produce. This is the essence of interpreting.

This basic understanding of how languages work is vital to anyone seeking to communicate effectively, and specifically to us as users of American Sign Language. All of us, having been raised in an English-speaking world, have all of our thoughts anchored to the English language. Therefore, to produce ASL properly, we must actually interpret our own thoughts to be reproduced in ASL instead of English. Arguably, there will be a time when one is fluent enough in ASL to produce messages directly from pure

4

thought without having to go through English to do it. However, this takes quite a bit of time. Therefore, you must think of yourself not only as an ASL user, but as an interpreter as well. The previous examples show the communication process as rather simplistic. However, there are other concerns which make it more complex. There are several levels to every language. These are as follows:

1   Tangible

This level represents all the physical things in the real world. Anything we can see, feel, taste, touch, or experience with our senses.

2   Ambiguous

This level represents ideas that have no physical representation, such as freedom, intelligence, or independence.

3   Emotional

This level represents feelings, such as happiness, anger, depression, gaiety, lightheartedness, rage, etc.

4   Idiomatic

This level represents words or phrases whose meanings are contrary to their literal meanings. Idioms are expressions like: It's as easy as falling off a log.

5   Poetic or Musical

This level represents the poetry or music of a language.

When we examine these various levels of language, it brings up

1

a new and interesting idea in our conceptual model thus far developed. When we looked earlier at how languages were developed, we said a group of individuals shared common experiences and wished to communicate. Therefore, they agreed upon a system of words and rules which allowed them to communicate. These groups of individuals we call cultures. A culture and its language are extremely interdependent.

The way we learn language now is not how it used to be. Today, we go to school and pick up a book with a myriad of confusing rules to memorize. But we must never forget how languages develop. Where did these rules come from? Who got together and made them up? No one did! The rules of language develop naturally from its use by its culture. *We* decide how our language is to be used. Languages work because they work. Meaning, they evolve through time, bending and shaping themselves for the use by the culture to more effectively communicate. English has changed drastically over the hundreds of years since its development. Why? Because we have changed our use of it. Our needs have changed, our expressions have changed, and thus the language has changed with us. So we must remember that a language is inseparably linked to the culture that formed and uses it.

This can be illustrated using the five levels of language. Every word has what we shall refer to as a dictionary definition. When we see the word "tree" we can look it up and there is an exact, and often exhausting meaning there for us. But words also have a cultural meaning, or cultural baggage, attached to them that often means more than the word itself. On the first level, the tangible level, we don t see this much. A tree is a tree, there isn't much the culture can do with an object that is there in the world minding its own business. These objects tend to fend for themselves, you might say. But start moving down the scale in the language levels and the meanings of words take on different baggage from culture to culture.

Let's look at the word "independence". In our American, English–speaking culture that word has some powerful baggage with it. It has a star-spangled-banner-symphony-in-the-background feeling to it. But in a communist culture, the word takes on a renegade feeling. Thus, even though the dictionary definition is the same between the cultures, the cultural meaning is not.

This is what is meant by the section of the code of ethics of the Registry of Interpreters for the Deaf (RID) which states we shall render the spirit and content of the message. The content is the dictionary definition, but the spirit is the cultural baggage that goes with that dictionary definition. The higher you go in the levels, the more weight spirit has over content, and

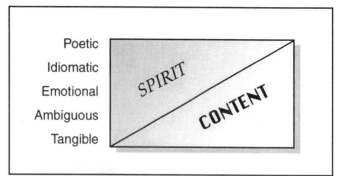

the greater the difference between the original and the interpretation. Let's take the most obvious of these examples, idiomatic phrases. Idioms are the most unusual things we have in language. These are phrases in which the intended meaning, or message conveyed, has absolutely nothing to do with the dictionary definition. On this level, even tangible objects are not immune to our cultural meddling. Let's look at the word "dog", for instance. Normally, this would be a very simple word. I have a picture of a cute, brown, furry, four-legged animal in my mind, and I want to convey it to you. I say "dog" and the deed is done.

But take it to the idiomatic level and we can do all kinds of things with it. If I am angry and have an angry voice and facial expression and yell "You dog!" then you are no longer seeing a cute, furry animal; you are being insulted. If we are talking about a date you had last night and we are both disgusting chauvinist pigs, I might say with a wicked grin, "You dirty dog", and you are being complimented on your enchanting ways with women. So, idioms can be very complicated.

Back to the example with an interpreter where you and I speak two different languages. This time, I speak German and you speak English. Again let's look at a simple, tangible object, such as a woman who does not work outside the home, but instead stays home to care for the family. In German I would say the word *"hausfrau."* The corresponding English would be house-wife. The dictionary definitions are identical, but there are cul-

7

tural differences. In German, the feeling or spirit of the word *"hausfrau"* is one of respect and admiration, but in English the term "housewife" is often looked down upon, or seen as old-fashioned. Therefore, the interpreter would have to look for a word with the same dictionary definition AND cultural meaning, such as "matriarch." An interpreter trying to convey the correct image to the consumer must have an intimate knowledge of not only the dictionary definitions, but also the cultural definitions of the words or phrases being used.

This is the biggest problem I have seen that students of ASL have. In general, any of us who have learned ASL have learned it in a similar way: the vocabulary method. We learned a one-to-one correspondence between an English word and its signed counterpart. This was effective to an extent because it aided in establishing the link between two representamen and one interpretant or object. However, this is only effective on the tangible level.

Many times we learned a one-to-one relationship that was not quite right. Each word or sign in any language has a certain scope to it, that is, its dictionary definition plus its cultural baggage. The scope from language to language can differ quite dramatically, such as in the example of "hausfrau" and "housewife." If we do not understand the differences between these words, we can cause miscommunication to occur.

In an example specific to ASL, let's look at the word "wrong" and the sign "WRONG." In English and ASL, the dictionary definition is the same. It is when something incorrect is said, done or occurs. But in English you have to ask yourself what is the feeling about this word? If I said the English phrase, "You're wrong," how do you feel? It not only judges your actions, it judges you as a person. It is insulting and belittling; it is an extremely strong phrase. In ASL you can produce the same message with an extremely negative facial expression and hard, fast signing of the phrase "WRONG-YOU." But this is rare. If a person neutrally signs "WRONG-YOU" there is no judgment of the person, no belittlement, no insult. The person this is signed to, instead of feeling judged, would simply look for a way to correct the error.

8

These types of cultural differences can and do often lead to terrible miscommunications and add to the misconception that the Deaf can be rude. The real problem is that as signers and/or interpreters we have erroneously linked certain words and signs as equal when they truly are not. Therefore, we must strive to always be conceptually accurate in our signing or interpreting, rendering both the spirit (the cultural baggage and feeling behind a word or concept) and the content (the dictionary definition) of each spoken or signed phrase.

As a final example, let's look at communication and interpreting as if we were delivering cargo on trains through Europe. Western Europe has a train system with standard rails. However, Eastern Europe and Russia have larger size rails that are farther apart than standard rails. This was done so that during war times, enemies could not ship supplies and troops via the train system. When cargo is being delivered across these borders, it must be unloaded from one kind of car and loaded onto another to make it to its destination.

Let's say we are in charge of a train that has precious cargo in it: food for starving people which we must deliver. Now let us consider what is most vital to our mission, the cars which are carrying the food, or the food itself? Well, of course it is the food: the cargo. When we reach the border we have a problem. We have to change the mode of our delivery. But this has been a long journey, and we have been with these cars for a very long time. We are familiar with them, and they have always worked well for us before. We have a loyalty to these cars and don't want to see them abandoned. Suppose we don't like the fact that we have to leave these cars behind and we decide to put rubber wheels on the cars and run them down the Russian lines between the tracks. (Imagine the gall of those people saying we have to change cars, hhmmpphh!) Well, we go bouncing down the track on our rubber wheels that we have quite cleverly fashioned for these cars of ours, and we finally get to the town of starving people.

We pull into town, quite pleased that we have delivered the cargo and were so clever to have kept our good and useful cars

1

as well, only to discover that our cargo was bounced and trounced all the way, throwing most of it out the windows and rendering the remainder practically useless; just a few scraps of lettuce left with which the people try to make a meal.

This is very similar to signing and interpreting. We have trains of words strung together to form sentences which carry a precious cargo of concepts. We are charged, as signers or interpreters, with delivering these concepts to those on the other side of the communication border. We learn, we sign, we practice, and we become Communication Engineers. We have studied hard and made a link for every English word we know.

Now we have a very important task. A sentence comes our way full of mental nourishment. What a great cargo! We prepare to cross the border, but find we have to switch from our wonderful English words that have always done a very fine job in the past to some strange and unusual patterns. The signs don't seem to want to link up in the nice English way; there is something definitely wrong here. Well, we rely on our knowledge that English is a wonderful language, and we stuff and force the conceptual cargo in whatever way we choose. We cut and snip where it doesn't quite fit, and we shove the signs or words to make them go together. We get the cargo on the newly designed train, which we are quite pleased with, and go on our way, delivering this wonderful sentence with a great sense of satisfaction. However, when the moment arrives and we open the doors for this great and glorious sentence to be displayed and communication to occur, we find that our content and meaning has all been destroyed. It has been bounced and trounced, stuffed and fluffed until it was nothing at all like it started out to be. In fact it isn't beautiful at all. Just a few scraps of meaning here and there with which the people can try to make a concept.

In a humorous way, what I am trying to impress upon you is the importance of conceptual accuracy and of conveying concepts (cargo) not just words (train cars). We as communication engineers hold the key to effective communication. We decide whether the mental nourishment will arrive as intended or not. We can be willful and prideful and force the language to meet

10

our comfort levels and beliefs, or we can learn to become the true linguistic experts we sell ourselves to be and learn all methods of communication and transference. We can become highly skilled in all areas and modalities of sign and learn to speak English in a professional and presentational manner. It is our duty to convey the most precious of human gifts: communication.

I hope that you will glimpse the importance and the beauty of what we do. If your goal in learning ASL is simply to become fluent in it, changing the paradigm you have of language and exhibiting a willingness to accept ASL as it is will be the first step towards fluency. If you would like to go on and become a professional intepreter, I hope you can embrace ASL as a language, learning it as well as is possible, and in doing so commit to becoming the most effective resource available to your profession.

ASL as a Visual Language

Now that you have been introduced to the concept of language development and use in the communication process, it is time to turn our attention specifically to American Sign Language (ASL). ASL is unlike any spoken language in existence. When we look at most spoken languages, they are highly dependent on word order and syntax to convey specific meaning. For instance, the English sentences, "The boy sat on the elephant" and, "The elephant sat on the boy" conjure up very different images based exclusively upon the word order.

ASL, however, is not as dependent on word order. In order to properly produce ASL concepts, we must change our way of thinking about how language works. In ASL, we are dependent upon the visual representation of concepts in a three dimensional space, not a linear progression of words. Spoken languages are dependent upon word order and voice intonation because of the mode of transmission. Our ears can only pick up one word at a time, followed by another. Therefore, this linear principle is not only prudent, but vital to the communication process. In fact, as spoken languages have progressed, we have taken linear sound to an amazing degree of complexity, introducing intonation, the ability to change meaning by stressing a certain word, and even creating complex systems such as sarcasm and jest by altering our tone of voice.

ASL, on the other hand, is received visually. Our audience sees with much greater detail than one can hear. In the same way spoken languages have developed in auditory complexity, ASL has developed within the visual dimension. ASL uses three dimensions and makes meaning of spatial relationships, movement, speed, and size of signs. And of course, since ASL is a living, evolving language, the complexity and use of space has increased through its usage by the culture in which it was created. One of the greatest weaknesses students of ASL have is in changing their perception of language into ASL's three dimensions as opposed to the linear progression of English or other spoken languages. When we try to dissect ASL and reproduce it in our mental image of linear English, what comes out is a bland, flat, boring stream of signs. And to those who use the full, three

13

dimensional complexity of the language, watching this can be quite tedious.

One way to begin to see the three dimensional or visual aspects of ASL is to think of signing as a creative process. When you sign something in front of you, you must imagine that you are not merely putting signs together in a linear order, but you are recreating the image in the space in front of you. Imagine yourself to be an all-powerful genie in charge of creating your own universe in front of you. You can create or destroy anything you choose. When you sign HOUSE, it appears in space before you the moment you sign it. If you want it to be rained on, burnt down, painted, or lived in, you simply have to sign it and it is so. Any event you want to portray can be created in your world in front of you. You choose the placement and direction of movement of the signs you use to show relationships among objects and events.

This creation of visual elements in the space in front of you is not just a concept in your mind as the signer. The receiver of the message is also relying on the image placed in your signing space to receive all the information you are trying to portray. They also see the house and all the events which happen in it or to it as you sign them. Therefore, if these objects or concepts are placed in your signing space in a linear fashion, with no focus on how they relate to each other, many misunderstandings may occur.

Using this image of creation will also help you understand and follow the rules which apply to sign placement and directionality in ASL. These rules are mostly rules of the physical and logical world as they apply to real objects. For example, in the real world a person cannot walk through the walls of a house, or a road cannot run through the base of a tree. These rules also apply to your signing of a concept in the space in front of you. The signed images that you create of objects, events, and relationships must follow the same physical rules that apply in the real world.

If you can begin to grasp this concept, that the signs you produce not only cause a mental image to appear in the mind of the

14

receiver, but also take on an almost physical property in the space in front of you, you are well on your way to creating a correct model in your mind of how ASL works.

These logical and physical rules we have mentioned are what we refer to as reality rules. We can't break the rules of reality. Therefore, when we are building a concept in front of us, we must do so following certain basic guidelines. Let's look at an example in the real world. Say you want to build a house (see illustration previous page). To do so you must follow certain steps. First a foundation must be dug, then the floor must be built, followed by the construction and raising of the walls, and finally the roof. After all this is completed you can then add on the details of windows, doors, and furnishings. To think that we could put a roof on without the walls, or the walls without a floor would be ludicrous. We know the logical steps of building a house.

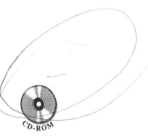

The same is true when building a signed concept in space. There are logical rules which must be followed. If we were describing a scene using ASL in which a young boy is sitting on a dock dangling his feet in the water we would have to do so in a logical order. Obviously you can't have a dock without a lake, you can't have a boy sitting on a dock that's not there, and you can't have feet dangling in water that's not there. So we describe a lake first, followed by the dock, followed by the boy, with the added description of the spatial relationship of the boy to the water and the dock. Keeping in mind that we must adhere to logical rules of creation will help in the correct usage of ASL. Here are the basic reality rules that we must follow:

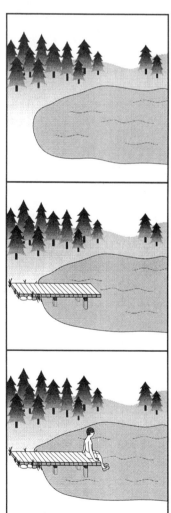

1 General to Specific (or General to Detailed)

When building our concept, we begin with the big picture, the background, and then add the details, much as we did when building our house. Another example is an artist who begins his painting with large sections of colored background, such as the sky or the ocean, and ends with the finest of details, like the leaves on the trees, or twigs in a bird's nest. Each object relates

15

2

to the ones before it. This is how we sign in ASL. Like our scene with the boy and the lake, we must begin with the largest background, the lake, and end with the smallest detail of exactly how the boy is sitting with his feet dangling in the water.

2 Concrete Before Abstract

This rule is similar to the General to Detailed rule. This rule states that you must have objects in place in your space before any actions can occur. For example, a man can't walk until he exists, a chair can't be sat upon until it exists in your space. So in the English phrase,"Three bears lived in a cottage in the woods," you would first establish the woods, then the cottage, then the three bears, and then the abstract idea of them living there. The woods, cottage, and bears are concrete tangible objects, whereas living is an abstract action.

This also applies to attributes. If you say in English, "The rose is beautiful," you have essentially two pieces of information. You have a rose and the fact that it is beautiful. Following our rule, we must place the rose in our space before the abstract concept of beauty can be attributed to it. Only objects can exist in our space independent of other information. Abstract ideas usually do not exist by themselves.

3 Spatial Relationships

In ASL, we must use spatial relationships as they exist in the real world. In English we say, "The ball is in the box." However, when we sign this, we must be careful. If we sign BALL first, as in the English word order, it is now existing in the space in front of us. How are we then going to sign that there is a box around it? If we sign BOX in the same space as the ball, we violate a basic space rule that no two things can exist in the same place at the same time. Therefore to sign this correctly we have to sign that first the box exists, and then that inside it is a ball. This is true of all prepositions: in, on, under, behind, etc. You must be very careful when signing prepositional phrases because more

16

often than not, the object of the preposition is signed before the preposition itself.

The Spatial Relationship rule also applies to ASL verbs. Verbs in ASL, as in English, show action. If the verbs are ones that move or show movement, you have to make sure the direction of movement makes sense within your signed concept and does not violate any spatial rules. For

instance, if you establish a house to the left of your body and you want to have a person move towards it, you can't have the person start at the center of your space and move to the right. The person would then be walking away from the house. If you have established a hill rising to your right and then have a person walk straight through that area, the person is walking through the base of your hill, and unless there is a tunnel there, that can't happen. So when placing objects in space, or when using verbs, we must abide by the reality rule of correct spatial relationships.

4 Chronological Order

In English, we say things like "I got scared when the dog barked at me." However, when we look at the actual series of events portrayed in this sentence, we find that first the dog barked at me, and then I felt afraid. In ASL, because we are recreating the scene in space, we must do so in the order the events actually took place. Therefore, if I were signing this, I would have to first place the person and the dog in the space (following the Concrete before Abstract rule), then show the action of the dog, and then my reaction to it.

Review:

All four of our "Reality Rules" are really just stating the fact that

2

with ASL, the concepts that we sign in the space in front of us must act as much like the real world as possible. We must move from the general, large objects to the smaller specific details. We must also make sure that the concrete objects are placed in our space before any abstract concepts are related to them, or before any actions occur. And finally, we must make sure that any actions that occur progress chronologically, just as they do in the real world, and also ensure that those actions do not violate any rules of reality, such as walking through walls.

Example:

Let's look at an example of how all of these rules come into play, examining only the conceptual order of the signed sentence and not necessarily the production of the signs themselves. Here's the sentence:

The clock in the living room has a pendulum with our family crest engraved on it.

When we look at this sentence there are really no action verbs, just a linking verb, which we will talk about later. Therefore, we are dealing with a description of several objects in relation to each other.

We have: a living room, a clock, a pendulum, and a family crest. The sentence is already set up in order from general to specific, we have the living room and a clock, all the other information are details of the clock itself. First we would establish the living room and a clock somewhere in it. We would then sign the pendulum making sure it is in the proper relationship to the clock. Finally we would reference a specific part of the pendulum and describe the family crest engraved upon it. From this example you can see that we work in ever increasing levels of detail, almost as if moving in from a distance with a close-up camera. This is how most sentences are signed in ASL.

The Use of Your Signing Space

Now that we have some idea of the rules used to portray concepts within our signing space, let's look at the logistical use of the space itself. Your signing space reaches from just above your head to approximately your waist, and about a foot on either side of you. Almost all signs are produced within this space. There are also rules governing the use of this space.

When you place objects in space in front of you in the signing process, they are traditionally placed either slightly to the left or right, not directly in front of the body. This space directly in front of you and slightly less than the width of your body is called the Sight Line. The Sight Line has very specific purposes, such as to show ownership or for direct discourse, which we will discuss later. Remember too that these objects take on an almost physical quality and placing them right in front of you would block your line of sight. So when placing objects in your signing space, make sure that you do so on either side of your Sight Line.

Conclusion:

If you follow these rules and begin to see ASL not as a linear progression of signs, but as a three dimensional, visual, and creative process, it will make your signing much more effective and improve your ability to truly understand how the language works. It is also vital to understand that this is a powerful language which can portray concepts in a way very different from that of spoken languages.

All of the rules in this chapter can be said to be rules for setting the stage. So review the rules in this chapter and then move on to the following exercises. If you need help, see the Answer Key.

2

Setting the Stage

Exercises

Directions:

Please read each sentence and write the correct ASL interpretation below it, putting the signs in order to produce a conceptually accurate image. Practice each sentence by signing it three or four times. If you would like to see how the sentence is signed, you can watch it on the accompanying CD-ROM.

Example:

The cat is in the tree.

TREE CAT THERE

(**THERE** in this case refers to pointing to the part of the tree the cat is in. Don't be too concerned with this, we will discuss it more later. Work more on simply putting the signs in the correct order.)

1   *I live on Main Street in New York.*

2   *The man sat on the chair in the living room.*

3   *The girl is in the class on the third floor.*

4   *The boy likes to play on the swing in the park by the lake.*

5   *The bears live in a cottage in the forest.*

6   *The towels are in the closet by the bathroom upstairs.*

7   *The clothes are in the dryer in the laundry room.*

8   *The plants are on the windowsill in the kitchen.*

9   *The papers are in the desk in the middle drawer.*

10   *The scissors are on the sink in the bathroom.*

Setting the Stage

Answer Key

1 *I live on Main Street in New York.*

NEW YORK, MAIN STREET, I LIVE THERE

New York is the backdrop, or the most general, of all the items, thus it is signed first. Main street is the next level of detail. Finally the last object "I" is placed followed by the abstract concept of living.

2 *The man sat on the chair in the living room.*

LIVING ROOM, CHAIR, MAN SIT (ON LOCATION OF WHERE CHAIR WAS PLACED.)

3 *The girl is in the class on the third floor.*

THIRD FLOOR, CLASS, GIRL THERE

4 *The boy likes to play on the swing in the park by the lake.*

LAKE, PARK, SWING, BOY, SWING, LIKE

This one is a little complicated but follows the same principle. The General to Specific rule, or Concrete Before Abstract will apply with the order of objects from largest to smallest all the way down to the level of the boy. Then the chronological order rule comes in causing the boy to play first and then like it.

5   The bears live in a cottage in the forest.

FOREST, COTTAGE, BEARS LIVE THERE

6   The towels are in the closet by the bathroom upstairs.

UPSTAIRS, BATHROOM, NEXT-TO, DOOR, OPEN, TOWELS THERE

7   The clothes are in the dryer in the laundry room.

LAUNDRY ROOM, DRYER, CLOTHES INSIDE

8   The plants are on the windowsill in the kitchen.

KITCHEN, WINDOW, SILL, PLANTS THERE

9   The papers are in the desk in the middle drawer.

DESK, MIDDLE DRAWER, PAPERS THERE

10 The scissors are on the sink in the bathroom.

BATHROOM, SINK, SCISSORS THERE

Chapter

3

Now that we have discussed the three dimensional aspects of ASL, we will begin discussing some of the mechanics of how we build concepts using ASL. One piece of information which is vital to all communication is when the actions we are portraying took place. This is referred to as tense. When we take this idea and apply it to ASL we must view it in the perspective of three dimensional language.

We have talked about how we decide which information is placed in our space first. We relied on rules like General to Specific, and Concrete before Abstract to help us do this. When referring to tense, we again have to see it as a part of the scene we are creating. Imagine yourself at a theater and on stage a scene is laid out. There are various objects placed about the stage, as well as people. There is also the backdrop or scenery which helps add to the atmosphere of the scene. Usually you will also be given information as to when the actions are taking place. Defining the moment in time when the actions occurred is really the whole role of tense in any language.

Seeing tense as part of the scenery of our concept helps us to understand how we are going to sign it. Tense in ASL is unlike that of English. In English and other spoken languages tense is indicated by the conjugation of verbs. For instance, we conjugate the verb "run" into "ran" to show the past tense. In ASL tense is not indicated by any change in the verb, but is instead shown by certain tense indicators.

Remember that we said that ASL has the ability to portray a scene in space. Whatever time you establish for that scene, much like the scene on the stage, becomes the tense for the entire duration of that scene. For instance, if you introduce your scene by signing "July 4, 1776," and then go on to describe certain events, it will be obvious that all the events in that scene are in the past tense. Similarly, if you start your signed sentence with the word "TOMORROW" it indicates that all the events are in the future tense.

ASL has two types of tense indicators: specific and general. Specific time indicators point you to a specific point in time such as YESTERDAY, TOMORROW, LAST YEAR, July 4, 1776 and

Tense Indicators...	
Specific	**General**
Yesterday	Before
Tomorrow	Ago
Last year	Now
July 4, 1776	Will
2:00 p.m.	After

25

3

2:00 p.m. Some of these name a very specific moment (2:00 pm), while others give you a range of time (last year) but all of these are considered specific time indicators. General time indicators are signs that only refer to the general past, present, or future. These include BEFORE (or AGO), NOW, and WILL. These signs only give you a very general time reference, not a specific point in time.

The rules in ASL for using tense indicators are relatively simple. You usually put a specific time indicator at the beginning of your sentence and a general time indicator at the end. Most often you will see them both in one sentence to emphasize the time reference. For example in the sentence, "I am going to the store tomorrow," you would see TOMORROW signed at the beginning as well as the WILL sign at the end.

It is rare to see general tense indicators at the beginning of a signed sentence, but at times you will. These are somewhat special cases when words like "someday" or "a long time ago" are used. These are specialized general tense indicators.

When using a specific tense indicator that refers to the past, such as YESTERDAY, LAST YEAR, or July 4, 1776, you will also see a special sign come into play later in the sentence. This sign is called the FINISH sign. It is very important to understand that this does not always equate to the English verb "to finish" meaning to complete. The sign FINISH plays the role of a tense indicator showing that an action has been completed. So in reference to our tense indicators, when you have a specific tense indicator at the beginning of your sentence which refers to the past , you will also see the FINISH sign before the verb. Let's look at an example:

ENGLISH: Yesterday I went to the store.

ASL: YESTERDAY, I FINISH GO-TO STORE I

This use of FINISH simply emphasizes the past tense of the sentence and is not considered to be required, but will turn up more

---

**Future
Tense
Sentence...**

"You usually put a specific time indicator at the beginning of your sentence and a general time indicator at the end."

Tomorrow *I GO STORE* Will

---

often than not.

In our above example, the sign FINISH acted on the verb TO GO to make it past tense. Sometimes you will see the FINISH sign after the verb phrase. In this case FINISH functions like the English word "already". For example, if we signed the sentence:

I GO-TO STORE FINISH I

we are placing special emphasis on the FINISH sign, and the English translation would be: "I already went to the store."

You will see this principle often in ASL: signs that are placed closer to the end of the sentence carry a special emphasis. Let's look at a few examples of how to use our tense indicators.

Example 1:

English: *Tomorrow I will go to the doctor.*

ASL: **TOMORROW I GO-TO DOCTOR WILL I**

Here we have a specific tense indicator at the beginning of a sentence which refers to the future, and so we will see the corresponding general tense indicator for the future tense at the end.

Example 2:

English: *Yesterday I went to school.*

ASL: **YESTERDAY I FINISH GO-TO SCHOOL I**

Here we have a specific tense indicator at the beginning of a

The Art of Interpreting *American Sign Language*

sentence referring to the past tense, and so we will have the sign FINISH before the verb.

Example 3:

> *English:*   *I bought some bread.*
>
> **ASL:**   **I FINISH BUY BREAD**

Here we have no specific tense indicator and so the FINISH sign indicates the past tense of the verb.

Example 4:

> *English:*   *I already bought the bread.*
>
> **ASL:**   **BREAD I BUY FINISH I**

Just as the English sentence changes its meaning with the word "already," moving the FINISH sign to the end of the sentence accomplishes the same thing in ASL.

Example 5:

> *English:*   *Someday I'll go to Rome.*
>
> **ASL:**   **WILL(SIGNED IN TWO FORWARD MOVEMENTS TO INDICATE FAR INTO THE FUTURE) I GO-TO ROME WILL I.**

In this case the general time indicator is at the beginning of the sentence, though its movement is modified to show the distant future.

Do not assume that all English words which seem like specific time indicators really are. For example, let's look at the English sentence, "I don't want to go to school tomorrow." This sen-

28

tence contains the word "tomorrow" which may appear to be a specific tense indicator. But the tense of this sentence is present, not future. The feeling of not wanting to go to school is happening right now. Therefore if we sign the sentence:

TOMORROW I GO-TO SCHOOL DON'T-WANT

we are really saying, "I won't want to go to school tomorrow." So in this case the word tomorrow is actually functioning as an adverb, not a tense indicator. The correct way to sign this sentence would be:

I GO-TO SCHOOL TOMORROW DON'T-WANT I

Please note that in these examples you shouldn't be too concerned about how the other signs are put into correct order. We will discuss that in the next chapters. Here we are simply focusing on the correct placement of the tense indicators.

It is also important to note that there are certain rules to follow when producing tense indicator signs regarding time.

1   All tense indicators which refer to a specific hour, such as

2:00 pm, must be signed: TIME 2

Examples:	*3:30*	*TIME 3 30*
	1:15	*TIME 1 15*

2   Any tense indicators which refer to a day occurring next or last week should be signed with NEXT/LAST WEEK first and the day second. Also note that you must include the full sign NEXT/LAST WEEK and not just NEXT or LAST.

3

Examples:

Next Wednesday

NEXT WEEK WEDNESDAY

Last Saturday

LAST WEEK SATURDAY

3 Any tense indicator referring to a month or season with a NEXT, LAST, or EVERY prefix must follow the same format as NEXT/LAST WEEK

Examples:

Next January

NEXT YEAR JANUARY

Last April

LAST YEAR APRIL

Last Spring

LAST YEAR SPRING

Every Summer

EVERY YEAR SUMMER

Now that we have looked at how to use tense indicators, let's try a few exercises.

The Art of Interpreting *American Sign Language*

NOTES

3

Tense Indicators

Exercises

Directions:

Using the space below each sentence, write the correct word order for each sentence as it would appear in ASL. Do not worry about the order of signs other than the tense indicators and what we have learned in previous chapters. If you would like to see how the sentence is signed, you can watch it on the accompanying CD-ROM.

1   I went to the doctor yesterday.

2   I missed my class last Wednesday.

3   We go to Disney World every summer.

4   Last month we were late paying rent.

5   Next year the convention will be in New York.

6   *I am going to Washington, D.C., next Saturday.*

7   *We went to church last Sunday.*

8   *The meeting will be tomorrow at ten.*

9   *Someday I want to go to Egypt.*

10 *Once upon a time a bear lived in a cottage in the woods.*

Tense Indicators

Answer Key

Please note:

The answers below may appear to violate the Concrete Before Abstract rule because the verbs are signed before the objects. However, this is because of the kind of verb being used in these examples. We will discuss these verbs later.

1   *I went to the doctor yesterday.*

    YESTERDAY I FINISH GO-TO DOCTOR

2   *I missed my class last Wednesday.*

    LAST WEEK WEDNESDAY I GO CLASS NOT I

3   *We go to Disney World every summer.*

    EVERY YEAR SUMMER WE GO-GO DISNEY WORLD

4   *Last month we were late paying rent.*

    LAST MONTH WE PAY RENT LATE I

5   *Next year the convention will be in New York.*

    NEXT YEAR CONVENTION THERE NEW YORK WILL

6   *I am going to Washington, D.C., next Saturday.*

**NEXT WEEK SATURDAY I GO-TO WASHINGTON D.C.
WILL I**

7   *We went to church last Sunday.*

LAST WEEK SUNDAY WE FINISH GO-TO CHURCH

8   *The meeting will be tomorrow at ten.*

TOMORROW TIME 10 MEETING WILL

9   *Someday I want to go to Egypt.*

WILL (DOUBLED) I GO-TO EGYPT WANT I

10 *Once upon a time a bear lived in a cottage in the woods.*

BEFORE (DOUBLED) WOODS COTTAGE BEAR LIVE THERE

The Art of Interpreting *American Sign Language*

Establishing Topic

Now that we have begun to grasp the nature of establishing the scene using tense indicators and basic objects, we are going to use these skills to establish topics in ASL sentences. The topic of an ASL sentence is similar in many ways to the subject of an English sentence; it is what all the other information relates to. However, this is not always the case in ASL, so we need to look specifically at what role the topic of an ASL sentence plays.

The topic of an ASL sentence is almost always a noun, or object. When we begin an ASL sentence, we have empty space in front of us. This space has no surfaces, no ground, it is simply a void. The topic of a signed concept provides the object or idea to which all the other information refers or relates in our three dimensional space. Therefore, the topic is usually the object which acts, or is acted upon in a sentence.

As we mentioned previously, in English, conceptual relationships are provided to us by the order of the words. To use a previous example, "The boy sat on the elephant," and "The elephant sat on the boy" create completely different mental images. The relationship between two objects (the act of sitting), and the preposition "on" work together to give us the complete meaning.

However, when we look at these examples in ASL, we find that the English subject is not the ASL topic. Let's look at the sentence "The boy sat on the elephant." In this sentence we have two objects which could be candidates for the topic of the sentence. If we use "boy" as the topic we run into a problem. If we first place the boy in space, we then have the problem of getting the elephant under him. Also, the verb, working with the preposition, points conceptually to the elephant, not the boy. All of these clues tell us that the elephant is the topic to which all the other objects refer to and interact with, so the sentence would be signed:

ELEPHANT, BOY SAT-ON

Signing the sentence in this manner sets the initial scene with the elephant, then establishes the second object, and then defines

4

their relationship. In most simple declarative sentences with two objects in relation to each other, you will find this order: Object, Object, Relationship.

Another type of simple declarative sentence has a single object and an attribute of that object. For example, the sentence, "The girl is pretty." This sentence tells us that there is a particular girl whose looks are considered by the speaker to be pretty. There is only one object in the sentence, the girl, so by default she will be the topic of our sentence. There are also other rules which tell us that the girl must be signed first, such as concrete before abstract. The girl is a tangible object while the attribute of prettiness is only a concept, therefore it is considered abstract.

Object, Object, Relationship

The first sign we would produce in this sentence would be GIRL, followed by her immediate placement in space. This is most usually done by pointing in the space where the girl will be placed, either slightly to the left or right of center to avoid the sight line. You can also place the sign GIRL in space by slightly turning your torso to the left or right while signing GIRL, though this is also usually accompanied by a reference such as pointing.

Next you want to communicate what she will do, or something about her that you are trying to communicate. We are simply going to assign an attribute to her, which we do by signing PRETTY, re-referencing or pointing back to the area where we placed the girl.

So the order of the signs in the sentence would be:

GIRL (POINT RIGHT) PRETTY (POINT RIGHT).

Use of Non-Manuals:

Now that we have the order of the signs to build this concept, it is important to understand that more than just signs are involved in any concept. There are also important non-manual features that create meaning. Non-manuals refer to anything that is part of the signed message, that creates meaning, that is not produced by the hands. These would include facial expression, eye gaze, pauses, shoulder shift, and the speed and size of signs. Non-manuals either add to the grammatical structure of a sentence, identifying the "parts of speech" certain signs are playing, or they add adverbial information to the verb or adjective.

Non-manuals play an important role in establishing topic. Every topic is indicated non-manually in the same way. This non-manual is called the Topic Indicator (TI). The first part of the TI is a facial expression, made by raising the eyebrows slightly in a questioning look. Second, the body is leaned forward slightly. Finally, just after the topic is signed, there is a slight pause before going on with the rest of the sentence, and reverting back to a natural facial expression and body position.

Using our example (The girl is pretty), we would include the TI this way:

> GIRL, POINT RIGHT, TI (EYEBROWS UP, BODY SLIGHTLY FORWARD, HELD FOR A MOMENT WITH A SLIGHT PAUSE) PRETTY (REVERT BACK TO NATURAL FACIAL EXPRESSION, BODY BACK INTO POSITION) POINT RIGHT.

This use of the TI is vital to the establishment of the topic in the minds of those with whom you are communicating. It is just as necessary as proper word order and punctuation in English.

The topic indicator is also used anytime you introduce another object into the sentence, though the first object is always considered to be the topic. The secondary objects also get a TI, but it is slightly less exaggerated. The eyebrows aren't quite as high, the body less forward, and the pause is shorter.

Another non-manual you will use in these types of simple declarative sentences is the head nod. Whenever you are stating something as a fact, the information following the objects, such as an adjective or the relationship between objects gets a slight head nod to indicate it is declarative. Taking this into account, after we finish placing the girl and finish the Topic Indicator, we

Non-manuals:...

Facial Expression
Eye Gaze
Pauses
Shoulder Shift
Speed & Size of Sign

CD-ROM

39

would revert back to a neutral stance and facial expression, and nod our heads while signing PRETTY and pointing back to the girl.

These non-manual features help keep the various signs in their proper roles. If we don't use non-manuals properly, it can lead to confusion. For instance, the topic indicator is identical to a yes-no question non-manual which we will discuss later. Therefore, if you hold the topic indicator too long in this sentence, it becomes a question: "Is the girl pretty?" By reverting to the head nod, with no raised eyebrows, it indicates a declarative sentence.

Let's look back at our sentence about the boy and the elephant. Using what we know now of non-manuals, the entire sentence would be:

>   *English:*   *The boy sat on the elephant.*
>
>   **ASL:**   **ELEPHANT (TI) BOY** (SLIGHT **TI**, REVERT BACK TO NEUTRAL STANCE AND EXPRESSION), **SAT-ON** (WHILE NODDING)

Another non-manual that you will use often is the VERY non-manual. In English we use words like "really" or "very" to show an increase in the intensification of an attribute. Through the use of non-manuals, ASL can do this without producing any additional signs. This is done by slightly exaggerating the facial expression, and slightly increasing the speed and size of the sign used for the attribute.

>   *English:*   *The girl is very pretty.*
>
>   **ASL:**   **GIRL (TI,** INDEX RIGHT**), PRETTY++** (WHILE NODDING)

PRETTY++ means the head nod is exaggerated slightly, the sign PRETTY is signed a little bigger and a little faster, and the eyes have more of an awed expression.

Non-manuals are vital to the communication process in ASL.

Many hearing students concentrate so much on sign vocabulary that they often forget the required non-manuals. We will pay special attention to these throughout our lessons.

Complex Topics:

Topics can often be more complex than a single noun. For example let's look at the sentence : "The girl in the red dress is pretty" Here we have a topic with more information about the girl than we had before. When an object (the girl) is followed by some part of speech modifying the object (in the red dress), the entire clause gets the topic indicator (TI). You treat a complex topic as if it is a complete sentence, following all the rules we've discussed. Therefore, the girl is signed first, followed by the red dress, with the Topic Indicator held throughout the entire topical clause. Then the attribute of prettiness is signed. This sentence would be signed as follows:

> **GIRL, TI,** INDEX RIGHT, PAUSE, **RED DRESS, TI** CONTINUES, INDEX RIGHT, PAUSE, BACK TO NEUTRAL STANCE, **PRETTY,** WHILE NODDING, INDEX RIGHT.

Finally, the last kind of topic you will encounter is when the topic is derived from a verb. This is unusual but it happens occasionally. For example, in the sentence, "Dancing is good exercise." The English verb "dancing" functions as a noun (a gerund) to become the subject of the sentence. In ASL, DANCING is considered an object when it is placed in your space just like "girl" in the previous example. All the other rules still apply as usual.

> *Dancing is good exercise.*

> **DANCING,** SIGNED TO RIGHT FOR PLACEMENT, **TI,** PAUSE, REVERT BACK TO NEUTRAL STANCE AND EXPRESSION, **GOOD EXERCISE,** WHILE NODDING.

Let's practice a few sentences and look at the variations you may run into. In the following examples, TI will mean the entire topic indicator, including facial expression, body movement, pause, and reverting back to neutral position and expression.

Example 1:

Jane is a good teacher.

In this example it may look like you have two objects, but in fact, JANE and TEACHER are actually the same person and therefore the same object. TEACHER in this case is just another name for JANE. Therefore it is signed like an attribute with no placement necessary.

JANE, TI, INDEX RIGHT, **GOOD TEACHER,** WHILE NODDING, INDEX RIGHT

Example 2:

The boy who made the cookies is nice.

Whenever you see a sentence which has a relative clause (who made the cookies), you use a sign in ASL called the SELF sign. A relative clause describes the noun it follows, as in the following:

The girl who made the dress

The house which is on the hill

The dog that played with the bone

Notice that these clauses all describe an *action* performed by the topic. Example 2 is a sentence with a complex topic and would be signed like this:

BOY, TI, INDEX RIGHT, **SELF (**SIGNED RIGHT**) BAKE COOKIES (TI** IS HELD THROUGHOUT**), NICE, PERSON HE** WHILE NODDING.

These are all the various topics you will encounter while signing. By following the rules of placement and the accompanying non-manual features, communicating declarative sentences will be easy. Using the rules we have discussed, complete the following exercise.

NOTES

The Art of Interpreting *American Sign Language*

4

Establishing Topic

Exercises

Directions:

Rewrite the following sentences in correct ASL grammar, including indication of topic indicator and non-manual features. Then sign each sentence several times focusing on the non-manual features of topic indication and head nod. If you would like to see how the sentence is signed, you can watch it on the accompanying CD-ROM.

1   That man is my teacher.

2   Jim is a good cook.

3   The woman in the blue dress is my mother.

4   The house with the white fence is mine.

5   The man who wrote the book is a good author.

6   Dancing is really fun.

7   *Bowling is very boring*

8   *Riding motorcycles is exciting.*

9   *Riding horses in the forest is dangerous.*

4

Establishing Topic

Answer key

1   *That man is my teacher.*

   THAT MAN, INDEX LOCATION OF MAN, **TI, MY TEACHER,** WHILE NODDING

2   *Jim is a good cook.*

   JIM, INDEX RIGHT, **COOK SKILL,** INDEX RIGHT, WHILE NODDING

Another way to say someone is good at something is to use the "skill" sign. When you use this sign, it goes after the verb.

3   *The woman in the blue dress is my mother.*

   WOMAN, TI, INDEX RIGHT, **BLUE DRESS, TI** HELD, INDEX RIGHT, **MY MOTHER,** INDEX RIGHT, WHILE NODDING

4   *The house with the white fence is mine.*

   HOUSE, TI, INDEX RIGHT, **WHITE FENCE,** SHOW LOCATION OF FENCE AROUND OR IN FRONT OF HOUSE, **TI** HELD, **MINE,** WHILE NODDING

5   *The man who wrote the book is a good author.*

   MAN, TI, INDEX RIGHT, **SELF WROTE BOOK, TI** HELD, **GOOD AUTHOR,** INDEX RIGHT, WHILE NODDING

6. *Dancing is really fun.*

DANCING, TI, INDEX RIGHT, **REALLY FUN,** WHILE NODDING

7 *Bowling is very boring.*

BOWLING, TI, VERY BORING, WHILE NODDING

Please note that in Examples 6 and 7 the adverbs REALLY and VERY can be produced non-manually instead of actually signing REALLY and VERY. This is done by exaggerating the facial expression and increasing the speed and size of the signs FUN or BORING.

8 *Riding motorcycles is exciting.*

MOTORCYCLE RIDE, SIGNED TO RIGHT, **TI, EXCITING,** WHILE NODDING

In this sentence "Riding motorcycles" has to be broken down. The motorcycle has to be signed first, then the action of riding it.

9 *Riding horses in the forest is dangerous.*

FOREST, HORSE, RIDE, ALL **TI, DANGEROUS,** WHILE NODDING.

In this sentence we have a very complex topic. We first must establish the forest, then the horse, and finally, riding it before we could sign the attribute, dangerous. Remember that the complex topic is treated as if it is its own complete sentence, and the rules for sentence-building are used.

Relationships Between Objects

So far, we have looked at setting the scene of a sentence using tense indicators and placement of objects and their attributes within our signing space. We then looked at how to establish the topic of a sentence, both in space and non-manually using the topic indicator. Now we are going to discuss the use of space for multiple objects, and how they relate to each other.

This leads us into a discussion of verbs. First, let's look at what verbs are. Verbs in English are defined as parts of speech that show action. Verbs in ASL are also used for this purpose. There is a class of verbs that are not strictly action verbs. These are called "to be" verbs. In English, "to be" verbs (is, am, are, was, etc.) show the existence of something, or are used in conjunction with other action verbs to show tense. Look at our example of, "The girl is pretty." Here the verb "is" simply shows the truth of the statement and assigns the attribute to the girl.

We already know how to establish tense, and also how to put objects in our space. So now let's concentrate on establishing clear relationships between objects using these "to be" verbs in conjunction with prepositional phrases and other verbs.

Let's look at a very basic example: "The jar is on the shelf." When we look at this sentence it creates a very specific picture in our minds. The verb "is" in this sentence simply shows the existence of the jar and establishes the present tense. Using our logic rules, we know that you have to have a shelf in existence before you can put anything on it. So the first thing we are going to do is sign SHELF, placing it on either the right or left of our sight line, with the topic indicator appropriately used.

Next we have to show the jar. Now because of how JAR is signed, we could simply sign it in the area above the shelf to get a general idea of the placement. However, the whole point of this sentence is to establish the relationship between the shelf and the jar. So we will sign the jar right in front of us, for later use.

This is one of the uses for our sight line. When we sign an object right in front of us, we are creating an image of it floating in "readiness" in front of us. This also allows us to manipulate the object before placing it. For example if our jar had a red stripe or specific writing on it, we could describe this in this ready position before we placed it in our space. So the jar is signed, with a secondary topic indicator, right in front of us, close to the body.

The third action is to then move the hand "holding" the jar up to the level of the surface of the shelf, letting our gaze follow. We leave the jar on the shelf, release the holding hand, and let the eyes remain for just a moment on the jar before looking back to the receiver of the message. This is what the sentence would look like.

> EXAMPLE: *The jar is on the shelf.*

SHELF, TI, JAR, SECONDARY **TI (PLACED IN FRONT OF THE BODY), ON**(SHOWN BY MOVING THE HOLDING HAND UP TO THE SHELF WHILE FOLLOWING THE JAR WITH YOUR EYE GAZE, RELEASING THE JAR ON THE SHELF, LEAVING EYE GAZE ON ON THE JAR FOR A MOMENT, AND RETURNING EYE GAZE TO RECEIVER)

This also follows the sign-order pattern we established previously of Object Object Relationship.

This may seem as if we are signing "I put the jar on the shelf," but this is not the case. In order to say this we would have to interject the sign "I" as well as take a more active posture in the placement of the jar. Without the "I" the action is not assigned to an individual and therefore is seen as just a mechanic of signing, and not as the verb "put."

Remember that all of these sentences we are signing are first thoughts in our minds. We are simply recreating that picture in space through the use of ASL. If you say the sentence "The jar is on the shelf" to yourself, and then compare the image in your mind with the one you have created in space, you will see they are identical.

As mentioned previously, when using prepositional phrases (on the shelf), the object of the preposition (shelf) will almost always be signed first in the sentence. Prepositions show relationships, like in, under, behind, beneath, etc. Therefore, according to our logical reality rules, the object of the preposition must already be established in space before anything can be in, on, or under it.

Classifiers:

Another set of tools we will use in this section are classifiers. A classifier is a sign that represents a set of objects, or a certain class of objects. For example, in English we have classifiers such as "hand-held tools," or "English-speaking people." These are labels that represent a whole group or category of items.

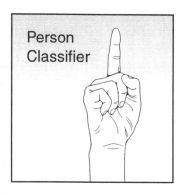

Person Classifier

In ASL there are two major classifiers which are used to describe people and vehicles. There are also certain additional descriptive hand shapes which are used to describe three-dimensional objects. The Person Classifier is the ONE hand shape. It is used to represent people and their movement or relationship throughout our space. The Vehicle Classifier is produced by using the THREE hand shape with the thumb pointing up and the fingers pointing forward. This is used to represent a car, boat, horse, or any other "vehicle."

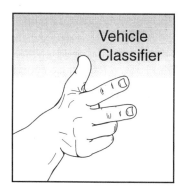

Vehicle Classifier

These two classifiers are extremely helpful in showing the relationship or movement of a person or vehicle as it moves around our space. We can show any kind of relationship, such as where the person is walking, what direction he is facing, and how he is moving throughout the space. With the vehicle classifier we can show turns, movement, or relationships as well.

The other classifiers are hand shapes which are used to describe similarly shaped objects. Here is a list of the most common ones:

Three-Dimensional Round Objects:

drinking glass, ball, tube, bowl, etc.

This is commonly called the C classifier because you use a "C" hand shape to describe the dimensions of the object.

51

Three-Dimensional Square Objects

box, shelf, stove, book, etc.

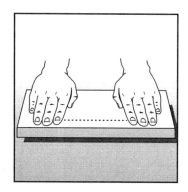

This is commonly called the B classifier because you use a flat handed "B" hand shape to describe the dimensions of the square object.

Two-Dimensional Flat Objects

check, license, certificate, etc.

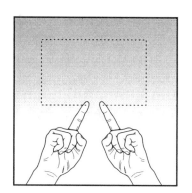

Usually used for paper objects, but can be used for other very thin, flat objects. This uses the two ONE fingers to "draw" the dimensions of the object.

Classifiers are almost like variables in math formulas, where X represents any number. The appropriate classifier can represent any person, car etc. To look at it another way, classifiers function much like English pronouns (he, she, it), taking the place of a noun you've previously mentioned.Classifiers are properly used by first naming the specific object and then placing the classifier in space to represent that object.The classifier then takes on all the attributes of an object or the persona of an individual.
Let's look at an example:

EXAMPLE:

The boy is standing behind the counter.

COUNTER (TI, PLACED ON RIGHT), BOY (TI, SIGNED IN FRONT OF BODY) CLASSIFIER: PERSON (PLACED BEHIND THE COUNTER, FACING TOWARDS THE SPEAKER, EYE GAZE TO THE PERSON CLASSIFIER)

Existential Have:

There is one additional way we can show relationships between two objects. This is called the existential have. When one object routinely has the other object in a standard relationship, we can say that one object "has" the other object. For instance, if I said, "There is milk in the refrigerator," this is a very normal relationship between the milk and the refrigerator. I could then sign this sentence: REFRIGERATOR HAVE MILK

This is very similar to the English usage of "have" in the sentence: "That store has good bread." You must be careful though only to use this technique in very standard relationships. Standard relationships are defined by where an object spends most of its time. Additionally, you use this when two inanimate objects are in the same sentence, not with a person and an inanimate object. For example, you could not use it to describe a person in a chair, saying CHAIR HAVE PERSON. Here are a few examples of where you could use the existential have:

Example 1

The clothes are in the dryer

DRYER HAVE CLOTHES IN (THE **IN** SIGN SHOWS THE RELATIONSHIP)

Example 2

There is a pendulum on the clock.

CLOCK HAVE PENDULUM (SHOW WHERE)

Example 3

There is a chair in the dining room.

DINING ROOM HAVE CHAIR (SHOW WHERE)

The Art of Interpreting *American Sign Language*

5

Here are some examples where it would not be appropriate:

1 *The people were standing in line.*

2 *The cat is under the bush.*

3 *The dog was in the street.*

Now we know more ways in which we can place and manipulate objects within our signing space. Using all of the principles you have learned, complete the following exercise.

NOTES

5

Relationships Between Objects

Exercises

Directions:

Rewrite the following sentences in correct ASL grammar, then sign each sentence several times practicing the establishment of spatial relationships. If you would like to see how the sentence is signed, you can watch it on the accompanying CD-ROM.

1   *The beer can is on the table.*

2   *The car is in the garage.*

3   *The people are standing in line.*

4   *There are two small potted plants on the shelf.*

5   *The woman is standing behind the counter.*

6   *The cat is under the stairs.*

7   The convention will be in Pittsburgh.

8   The Grand Canyon is in Arizona.

9   The car is parallel parking.

5

Relationships Between Objects

Answer Key

1 *The beer can is on the table.*

In this example we can use either the existential have, or simply the standard technique, though in all cases where you can, the use of the existential have is better.

> A. **TABLE (TI** PLACED RIGHT) **HAVE BEER CAN** (THEN SHOW THE RELATIONSHIP BETWEEN THE TABLE AND THE CAN BY MOVING THE **C** CLASSIFIER WHICH IS ALREADY FORMED BY THE SIGN **CAN** AND PLACING IT ON THE TABLE)

> B. **TABLE (TI,** PLACED RIGHT) **BEER CAN (TI** SIGNED IN FRONT OF BODY ON SIGHT LINE) **ON** (SHOWN BY MOVING THE "**C**" CLASSIFIER WHICH HAS ALREADY BEEN PRODUCED BY THE SIGN **CAN** TO THE POSITION ON THE TABLE, LETTING EYE GAZE FOLLOW, RELEASE CAN ON TABLE, LET EYE GAZE LINGER FOR A MOMENT, RETURN EYE GAZE TO AUDIENCE)

2 *The car is in the garage.*

> **CAR GARAGE (TI,** SIGNED RIGHT) (SIGN **CAR** FIRST, THEN SHOW THE RELATIONSHIP BY PLACING THE VEHICLE CLASSIFIER, SIGNED WITH RIGHT HAND, UNDER THE ROOF OF THE GARAGE, SIGNED WITH LEFT HAND). MAKE SURE YOU PLACE THE CAR IN THE GARAGE, DON'T SLIDE IT UNDER THE ROOF, THIS WOULD COMMUNICATE THAT THE CAR WAS DRIVEN INTO THE GARAGE.

3 *The people are standing in line.*

The Art of Interpreting *American Sign Language*

Here we will use a variation of the PERSON classifier. To show people in a line, use the FOUR hand on both hands so it looks like there are four people on both hands. Then you place the right hand forward with the left hand behind it, lining the fingers up all in one row, then you slide the left hand back to show a multiplication of people.

PEOPLE PEOPLE-LINE(CLASSIFIER AS DESCRIBED ABOVE)

4   There are two small potted plants on the shelf.

Here again it is best to use the HAVE sign.

SHELF (TI, PLACED WITH "B" CLASSIFIER)**HAVE PLANT**(SIGNED IN FRONT OF BODY, SIGNED SMALLER THAN USUAL WITH SHOULDER SLIGHTLY HUNCHED TO SHOW SIZE) **ON** (SHOWN BY BOTH HANDS IN "C" CLASSIFIER MOVING THE PLANTS JUST SIGNED FROM RIGHT IN FRONT OF YOU AND PLACING THE "POTS" ON THE SHELF)

5   The woman is standing behind the counter.

COUNTER (TI, PLACED WITH "B"CLASSIFIER) **WOMAN** (SIGNED IN CENTER OF SIGHT LINE, THEN THE **PERSON** CLASSIFIER IS PLACED BEHIND THE COUNTER FROM THE SPEAKER)

6   The cat is under the stairs.

STAIRS (SHOWN BY TWO FINGERS "WALKING" UP AN INCLINE THUS PLACING THE STAIRS) **CAT (TI) THERE** (POINT UNDER THE STAIRS)

Here it is best if you can sign double-handed. After your two fingers walk up the stairs, hold your "walking" fingers at the top of the stairs and then sign CAT and point under your "stairs". This makes it a little more clear.

59

7 The convention will be in Pittsburgh.

CONVENTION (TI) THERE (POINT RIGHT) PITTSBURGH WILL

8 The Grand Canyon is in Arizona.

GRAND CANYON (SPELLED) THERE (POINT RIGHT) ARIZONA

9 The car is parallel parking.

THIS SENTENCE IS SIGNED BY USING ONLY THE SIGN **CAR** AND TWO VEHICLE CLASSIFIERS. YOU FIRST SIGN **CAR**, THEN PLACE ONE VEHICLE CLASSIFIER WITH YOUR LEFT HAND AND LEAVE IT THERE THROUGHOUT. YOUR RIGHT HAND THEN FORMS A SECOND VEHICLE CLASSIFIER. YOU SHOW A CAR PULLING UP BESIDE THE PARKED LEFT HAND, AND BACK-ING UP INTO THE SPACE BEHIND IT, JUST AS YOU WOULD ACTUALLY SEE A CAR DO THIS. BE CAREFUL THAT YOU GO THROUGH ALL THE ACTUAL MOVEMENTS A CAR WOULD HAVE TO MAKE. DON'T SLIDE SIDEWAYS, CARS CAN'T DO THIS.

Non-directional Verbs

We have discussed how "to be" verbs (is, am, are, was, etc.) are generally used to show the existence of objects and their relationship to other objects. Now we are going to move into the true action verbs.

Verbs are one of the most significant parts of any language. Most information is relayed through verbs. Nouns or objects simply tell us that something exists and has certain attributes without supplying any further information. The verbs are where most of the communication comes in. Verbs establish relationships and interaction between objects, tell us what those objects are doing or what is being done to them. Therefore, it is vital to understand exactly how to correctly use verbs in ASL.

Before we go on with the discussion, we need to understand more about how ASL works, and what determines the topic of a sentence. In ASL, as we have stated, objects are placed in the scene first, then information about those objects is communicated, and finally any actions are shown. ASL tends to have the most important information in the sentence at the end. Therefore, you will see most verbs occurring towards the end of the sentence. This principle also helps us decide which objects come first in the ASL sentence.

We are going to divide ASL verbs into categories according to how much information they are capable of conveying. Some verbs can be modified in their movement to show not only the action that occured, but also several things about how it occured, like direction, and its subject and object. Other verbs can only name the action and can't be modified in their movement to provide any other information. These are called non-directional verbs. They are always signed the same way regardless of context. Some non-directional verbs are: (see right).

Again we have to look at this in terms of our three-dimensional space. The subject of a sentence is the object performing the action. The object of a sentence is the object being acted upon. These non-directional verbs (which cannot be modified in their movement to supply us with any other information) require both the subject and object to be expressly stated. For example, if we sign LOVE, we have no idea who is loving, or what is being

---

Non-directional Verbs...

Love
Want
Understand
Feel
Enjoy
Like
Admit
Think
Know
Remember
Explain
Summarize

6

loved. The verb itself supplies us with no information regarding what direction the love is moving. Therefore, to make the verb carry any pertinent information, we must state both who is loving, and who or what is being loved. Here are examples of different types of sentences that contain non-directional verbs.

Multiple Object Sentences:

Subject = I

Non-directional verbs may appear in sentences having two objects. For example, "I want a bike." In this sentence there are two objects, the person represented by "I" and the bike. The difficulty comes in when deciding which object should be placed in space first. You can sign the sentence with complete grammatical correctness several different ways:

1. **BIKE (TI, PLACE RIGHT) WANT I**

2. **BIKE (TI, PLACE RIGHT) I WANT**

3. **I WANT BIKE I**

Several things are going to affect how this sentence will be signed. The most common way this sentence will be signed is in example 1, BIKE WANT I. This follows all of our reality rules. Logically, you must have a bike established in space before you can want it. Placing "I" at the end of the sentence ties the emotion of wanting to you. You might think it odd that the bike is the topic and not "I". However, because the speaker has an actual physical presence in the signing space, it becomes less vital to establish "I" as the topic. And as we've mentioned, doing so brings the speaker into an usually high level of emphasis. You will see this is usually the case when the subject of the sentence is "I."

The second example (BIKE I WANT) changes the emphasis of

the sentence. As we said before, the most important information will be signed last in the sentence. This would be equivalent to the English sentence, "I *want* a bike." This changes the emphasis to the feeling of wanting the bike. The third example (I WANT BIKE I) shifts the emphasis off the bike and establishes "I" as the topic. This is highly unusual and would be equivalent in English to, "*I* want a bike!" Either you are expressing the fact that you want the bike as opposed to someone else, or you are a child throwing a tantrum in a toy store. The highly unusual practice of placing so much emphasis on the person rather than the object is shown by the format I WANT BIKE I.

These three examples show the effect of intonation or context on the expression of an ASL sentence. Spoken language users have the ability to change meaning through the use of intonation. The same is accomplished in ASL through this switching of sign order to place emphasis. By far the most common occurrence is that of example (1), but it is important to understand the various alternatives. Here are a few more examples:*

1   *I love ice cream.*

ICE CREAM, LOVE I

2   *I understand French.*

FRENCH LANGUAGE, UNDERSTAND I

3   *I enjoy classical music.*

CLASSICAL MUSIC, ENJOY I

*(Please note: In all of these examples, the comma after the topic indicates a topic indicator and a pause. This notation will be used throughout the remainder of the text.)

63

6

Subject ≠ I:

Suppose the subject of a multiple object sentence is not "I":
"Jim wants a bike." We will assume that we haven't talked
about Jim before, and therefore we must place him in our space
before we can talk about him.

Jim is really the topic of the sentence, the sentence is about him.
But what he wants is the most vital piece of information being
relayed. When you have a person as one object and an inanimate second object, the person will almost always get the topic
indicator. Now we have two options:

1. JIM, WANT BIKE HE

This is the normal way of singing this with no special
emphasis; or,

2. JIM, BIKE HE WANT IT

This is a little unusual, placing the emphasis on the wanting
instead of the bike.

Compare this with our "I want a bike" example. With "I" as the
topic, we have no way to establish "I" first without undue
emphasis. Therefore, the topic indicator automatically falls on
the bike, with the want following it. However, when we have
Jim as the subject, he automatically becomes the topic by
default. This frees up the bike to be placed at the end of the sentence where it normally would go, being the most important
piece of information in the sentence.

Subject = he/she/it:

To understand the sign order that would affect a sentence containing a pronoun, we have to understand the role of a pronoun. Pronouns act to take the place of nouns. However, when
you use a pronoun the noun has always been talked about first.
For example, if I say, "Jim got a new bike, he really likes it." He
and it both refer to objects that have already been introduced.

This is true in ASL as well. Any time you reference an object using a pronoun, that object must already have been placed in your signing space.

Therefore, when signing a sentence such as "He wants a bike," we must assume that the HE is already established as a known person in the signing space. The sentence would be signed:

HE WANT BIKE HE

The first HE establishes the person as the topic, the bike is placed near the end as the most important piece of information, and it is all wrapped up by re-referencing HE. Of course, in this sentence you have the option of placing WANT at the end for special emphasis, just as in our previous examples. Here are a few more examples:

1   *The man in the red hat wants a bike.*

   MAN, RED HAT, WANT BIKE HE

2   *That bike is fun. Jim wants it.*

   BIKE THAT FUN, JIM WANT IT

Here we have the bike as the first topic, placed in space and given an attribute. We then place Jim in space, apply a non-directional verb, and tie them together by referencing the bike.

There are several variations on these sentences depending on the emphasis of the speaker, but here are the basic summary rules:

SUBJECT = I
OBJECT (TI, Placed in space) VERB I

BIKE WANT I

SUBJECT ≠ I
TOPIC (TI, placed in space) VERB OBJECT

JIM WANT BIKE HE

SUBJECT = PRONOUN
PRONOUN VERB OBJECT PRONOUN

HE WANT BIKE HE

Single-Object Sentences:

Non-directional verbs can also act on other verbs, abstract nouns, adjectives or adverbs. In this example, an abstract noun refers to a word that is defined as a noun in English, but is not actually an object that takes up space. For example, "dog", "house", and "tree" are all objects. However, "independence", "Russian", and "freedom" are all nouns that are not objects; they don't take up space. Here are a few examples:

1   *(verb)*   *I love to dance.*

2   *(abstract noun)*   *I understand French.*

3   *(adjective or adverb)* *I feel sick.*

With verbs or nouns, the sentences are going to follow the same rules as with multiple object sentences. You will sign them the same way as the multiple object sentences, simply replacing the second object with the verb or abstract noun.

1   DANCE, LOVE I
   JIM LOVE DANCE HE
   HE LOVE DANCE HE

2 FRENCH LANGUAGE, UNDERSTAND I

JIM, UNDERSTAND FRENCH LANGUAGE, HE

SHE UNDERSTAND FRENCH SHE

Remember, even though these are not technically objects because they cannot take up space, they can be placed in space and act just like objects.

Adjectives and adverbs are almost never placed in space by themselves. Therefore, whenever you have a sentence with a non-directional verb that acts on an adjective or adverb, it will be signed exactly as it is stated in English.

1   I feel sick.

I FEEL SICK

Jim feels sick.

JIM FEEL SICK

He feels sick.

HE FEEL SICK HE

2   I remember nothing.

I REMEMBER NOTHING

Jim remembers nothing.

JIM REMEMBER NOTHING HE

She remembers nothing.

SHE REMEMBER NOTHING SHE

In all of these sentences, the adverbs "sick" and "nothing" cannot take up space as an object, therefore, they must always be placed at the end of the sentence.

Now you have all the rules needed for dealing with sentences containing non-directional verbs. Using the above rules, complete the following exercise.

NOTES

6

Non-directional Verbs

Exercises

Directions:

Using the examples and principles in the chapter, rewrite the following sentences in correct ASL grammar. Then practice signing each sentence utilizing the appropriate non-manual markers and spatial relationships. If you would like to see how the sentence is signed, you can watch it on the accompanying CD-ROM.

1 Sue feels sick.

2 He wants a new bike.

3 I understand Russian.

4 I want some chocolate ice cream.

5 I know John Smith.

6 I enjoy playing the piano.

7   *I remember that girl.*

8   *I like water skiing.*

6

Non-directional Verbs

Answer Key

1 *Sue feels sick.*

   SUE FEEL SICK

2 *He wants a new bike.*

   HE WANT NEW BIKE HE

In these and all other sentences the entire object "new bike" is considered a complex topic.

3 *I understand Russian.*

   RUSSIAN LANGUAGE UNDERSTAND I

4 *I want some chocolate ice cream.*

   CHOCOLATE ICE CREAM, WANT I

Here you have to omit the English usage of "some". It is understood in ASL.

5 *I know John Smith.*

   JOHN SMITH, I KNOW HE

6   *I enjoy playing the piano.*

   PLAY PIANO, ENJOY I

7   *I remember that girl.*

   THAT GIRL, I REMEMBER HER

8   *I like water skiing.*

   WATER SKI, LIKE I

Another kind of verb we want to discuss is the one-directional verb. These verbs differ from the other verbs we have discussed in the way they are produced and the information thay can convey. We said that with non-directional verbs, you have to explicitly state which object is acting, and which object is being acted upon. This is because the production of those verbs can't be modified. With one-directional verbs, the object that the verb is acting upon is identified by the verb itself. The verb is modified in its production to identify the object. Let's look at an example.

EXAMPLE:

I drove to Chicago.

In this sentence, let's assume that we have previously talked about Chicago, so we have it set up in space to our right. When we sign the verb DRIVE, it is going to originate from the space immediately in front of our bodies and move to the right to identify Chicago. If we had Chicago set up on our left, the verb would start at our bodies and move to the left. Therefore, one-directional verbs move to and identify the object they are acting upon.

It is very important that these one-directional verbs are utilized and produced correctly. The direction they move, just as word order in English, drastically affects the meaning of the sentence. Spatial relationships can get very tricky and must be clearly defined when using directional verbs.

One error that ASL students often make is equating English words to signs, and this can lead to difficulty in communication. For example, many of us learned the sign COME as two "one" hands moving towards our bodies, and GO as moving away from our body. However, if the English sentence is "I will come over to your house," and we sign COME towards us, it would completely misconstrue the direction. The motion should be away from the body, going in the direction where the house was established in space.

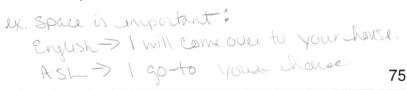

75

Proper use of one-directional verbs also comes into play when the verb acts on us as the signer. We often learn to produce a sign in one particular way. However, one-directional verbs often have a separate form to be used in reference to ourselves. Here are a few of these verbs: (see left)

In each of these examples, many signers start with the verb moving away from themselves and then point back to their bodies, trying to attribute the verb to themselves. This is a conceptual error. Each of these verbs should be signed beginning away from the body, moving in the opposite direction as usual, and ending with the verb directed toward the signer.

One-directional Verbs...
(referencing self)

Pay me
Tell me
Choose me
See me
Advise me
Ask me

Pay me:

Instead of beginning the sign at the base of the palm and moving out, it begins at the tip of the fingers, moves down the palm, and ends pointing at the signer.

Choose me:

The thumb and first finger should be pointed towards the speaker and then moves up and away from the body.

Advise me:

The movement of the dominant hand should be reversed, moving across the back of the non-dominant hand, fingers pointing *towards* the signer.

Tell me:

The first finger of the dominant hand starts away from the body, moves towards the signer, touches the chin, and ends pointing to the chest of the signer.

See me:

The SEE sign points towards the signer from the direction of the seeing person.

Ask me:

The question mark form of this sign is directed at the signer.

Another problem that occurs with these verbs is called double-indexing. Many signers will form the verb with the correct direction, but then after the verb, will point to themselves again. Because the verb has already identified the signer as the object of the verb, this is actually saying something like, "He told me me," and should be avoided.

There are three different kinds of one-directional verbs, each of which has its own specific rules governing its use. These are:

> *One-directional Travel Verbs*
>
> *One-directional Non-travel Verbs*
>
> *One-directional Object Verbs*
>
> *One-directional Travel Verbs:*

These verbs get their name because they all involve acts of traveling from one place to another. Here is a list of some of these verbs: (see right)

These verbs not only serve to identify the object of the verb, they also move the object that is being acted on from one place to another within your signing space.

One-directional Travel Verbs...
Drive
Go
Come
Walk
Run
Fly
Boat
Ride

EXAMPLE:

> *Jim flew to San Diego.*

CD-ROM

If we have Jim set up on the left and San Diego set up on the right, the verb actually moves Jim across our space so that he is on the right with San Diego. From this point on, all signs referring to or referencing Jim will now occur on the right, not left. The travel verbs are some of the most powerful signs we have in our vocabulary arsenal because of this transporting effect. However, they can be difficult if we are not practiced with their use. For instance, if we move Jim to our right and then reference him on our left in his old position we can really confuse the issue.

We can refer back to Jim on our left, but what we are indicating is a time before Jim flew to San Diego. We are traveling back in time. So we can have two Jims existing in two different times in our signing space. This isn't usually done, but it is a useful tool. However, usually when a person refers to the old position of the object, it is not intentional and can cause confusion.

Another powerful quality of these signs is that when moving an object from one place to another, they actually create a place for the object to go. The implication of a travel verb is that a traveling object must go somewhere. This affects the order in which we will sign the sentence. Let's look at this same, sample sentence: Jim flew to San Diego.

Let's assume that we haven't talked about Jim or San Diego before, so in the course of the sentence we are going to have to place both of these objects. Normally, both objects would have to be placed in space before we could have interaction between them. However, this is one of the properties of a travel verb. Let's look at how this would be signed:

STEP 1.   JIM (TI, PLACE LEFT)

This establishes Jim in space to our left and makes him the topic of our sentence. This makes sense since we already said that when you have a person and an inanimate object in the same sentence, the person will usually be the topic.

STEP 2. **FINISH FLY(** BEGINS AT LEFT AND MOVES TO THE EMPTY SPACE ON OUR RIGHT**)**

What we have done with this is picked up Jim and transported him to another location. Because of the nature of the sign, and because Jim had already been assigned a space, his space is taken with him. Therefore, when we drop him off on our right, we aren't leaving him in a void, but are instead transporting both him and his space to our right. The FINISH sign is used to establish the past tense of the verb.

STEP 3. **SAN DIEGO** (SIGNED OR SPELLED ON RIGHT IN NEW LOCATION OF JIM)

What we have done in this step is simply given a name to the new location of Jim. San Diego is not necessarily an object in this case, but rather a name of the location and environment, therefore it takes on a more abstract quality.

> **Topic, Verb, Object**

Through this example you can see that when using one-directional travel verbs, the sign order will be very similar to the English word order: TOPIC, VERB, OBJECT

EXAMPLE:

I went to the store.

I FINISH-GO STORE

The store can be established either to the right or left.

One interesting aspect of the travel verbs occurs when I is the subject. Instead of moving us as the speaker to the new location (the store in this case), the location is moved to us. It is like an instant scene change. Now anything we say or do will happen in the store.

How was this done?

Special Emphasis:

As with all of our examples so far, we have the ability to emphasize certain parts of the sentence by changing the sign order. For example, with any of the above examples, if we make the location the topic, we are drawing special attention to the location.

EXAMPLE:

Jim flew to San Diego. (as opposed to San Francisco)

SAN DIEGO, JIM FINISH FLY

If we wanted to emphasize the mode of travel, we would leave Jim as the topic, but then would place the location and finally the verb. This places the verb at then end, adding special emphasis to it.

EXAMPLE:

Jim flew to San Diego. (as opposed to driving)

JIM, SAN DIEGO, HE FINISH FLY

This concludes all the rules associated with one-directional travel verbs. Using the above examples, complete the following exercise.

NOTES

7

One-directional Travel Verbs

Exercises

Directions:

Using the principles and examples from this chapter, rewrite the following sentences in correct ASL grammar. Practice each one, signing it two or three times, utilizing correct direction and spatial relationships. If you would like to see how the sentence is signed, you can watch it on the accompanying CD-ROM.

1   Jane drove to Chicago.

2   I went to work.

3   Cheryl drove to Washington, D.C.

4   Ben came to my house.

5   My mom went to work.

6   Jeff walked to work.

7   Dad flew to San Antonio, Texas.

8   Bob and Sue went to the office.

9   Please come to my house.

One-directional Travel Verbs

Answer Key

1   *Jane drove to Chicago.*

    JANE, FINISH DRIVE CHICAGO

2   *I went to work.*

    I FINISH GO WORK

Here work is just like any other object and is placed in space.

3   *Cheryl drove to Washington, D.C.*

    CHERYL FINISH DRIVE WASHINGTON D.C.

4   *Ben came to my house.*

    BEN FINISH COME MY HOUSE

This is one of the few cases where we can place an object on the sight line. Because it is the signer's house, it will be placed in front of the body on the sight line. This equates you and your house. The only time this would not be true with this sentence is if it were obvious from the context that you were not at your house when Ben went there. Then you would want to place your house somewhere not associated with you.

5   *My mom went to work.*

MY MOTHER FINISH GO WORK

6   *Jeff walked to work.*

JEFF, WORK (PLACED OPPOSITE JEFF) **WALK**

Because this sentence implies a stress on the mode of transportation, it is modified to reflect this.

7   *Dad flew to San Antonio, Texas.*

MY FATHER FINISH FLY SAN ANTONIO TEXAS

Here, we must add the sign MY to FATHER because in ASL, when a person says Dad, it is not assumed to be MY dad as it is in English.

8   *Bob and Sue went to the office.*

BOB, SUE (BOTH PLACED IN THE SAME LOCATION) **FINISH GO OFFICE**

Here the classifier for the GO sign would be modified to use the first and second fingers, showing two people going as opposed to the normal ONE hand shape.

9   *Please come to my house.*

YOU COME MY HOUSE (PLEASE)

85

Here the subject of the English sentence, the understood "you," must be stated, and MY HOUSE would be signed in the center, close to the body. Additionally, "please" is usually shown non-manually, meaning through expression and demeanor, not through signing. Used in this context, "please" is an expression of the hearing culture and is not commonly used by the Deaf.

One-directional Non-travel Verbs

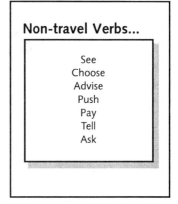

The next kind of one-directional verb we want to discuss is the non-travel verb. This verb acts like all other one-directional verbs in that it moves to and identifies the object of the verb. However, it is unlike the travel verb in that it does not transport objects across your signing space; this will affect the sign order. Here is a short list of non-travel verbs: (see right)

Because these verbs do not transport objects, the object the verb is acting on must be established before you can sign the verb. Remember that when Jim was flying to San Diego, we moved him and his space to the other side of our signing space, thus allowing us to sign San Diego last. Now, however, we don't have this transporting quality of the verb, so we must revert back to our typical method of signing multiple object sentences: Object, Object, Relationship (in this case a non-travel verb).

> **Non-travel Verbs...**
>
> See
> Choose
> Advise
> Push
> Pay
> Tell
> Ask

Example:

I saw the red light.

RED LIGHT (TI, PLACED IN CENTER ABOVE THE EYES OF THE SPEAKER, WHERE A RED LIGHT WOULD USUALLY BE) I FINISH SEE (THE FINGERS OF THE SEE SIGN MOVE UP AND POINT TO THE RED LIGHT)

Because the subject of the sentence is "I," the second object will be the topic, as we have seen in previous examples.

Example:

Jimmy told Jane.

JIMMY FINISH TELL JANE

In this case, we have two objects who are both people. This opens up more flexibility with the sign order. The order in which the objects are placed will decide which is the topic. This is up to the signer and the context of the situation. Most commonly, the

sign order in this case will go against the norm and place the object of the verb last.

Example:

He paid John.

JOHN, HE FINISH PAY

Here we have a case where one of the objects, a person, has already been established. In this case, the object of the verb is placed as the topic first, followed by the already-established object and then the verb. Again, you have a lot of flexibility depending on the emphasis of the sentence.

To summarize, one-directional non-travel verbs tend to be signed in our Object, Object, Relationship pattern, though it is easily flexible depending on emphasis.

NOTES

8

One-directional Non-travel Verbs

Exercise

Directions:

Rewrite the following sentences in correct ASL grammar. Practice signing each sentence three or four times focusing on spatial relationships and sign order. If you would like to see how the sentence is signed, you can watch it on the accompanying CD-ROM.

1   *I saw the red light.*

2   *I chose the blue dress for the party.*

3   *He advised me to take a math course.*

4   *Bob saw the boy riding his bike.*

5   *I saw that new French film.*

6   *He asked Jon for $10.00.*

7   *Please tell Mike to come home.*

8   *He asked the teacher.*

9.   *Billy pushed the girl.*

The Art of Interpreting *American Sign Language*

One-directional Non-Travel Verbs

Answer Key

1 *I saw the red light.*

   RED LIGHT, I FINISH SEE

2 *I chose the blue dress for the party.*

   BLUE DRESS, I FINISH CHOOSE FOR PARTY

This introduces a "for..." phrase. These are very flexible and can be put almost anywhere in the sentence. Usually they will be at the end of the sentence.

3 *He advised me to take a math course.*

   HE ADVISE-ME, TAKE MATH CLASS

4 *Bob saw the boy riding his bike.*

   BOY, BIKE, ON, BOB FINISH SEE

This is a little more complex because Bob saw an entire scene instead of just one object. Here, we look at the complex topic (the boy riding on his bike) and we have to build it on either our right or left as if the entire scene was just one object. We must follow all the rules for scene building while doing so. The boy is the topic, followed by the bike and then the relationship (object, object, relationship).

5   *I saw that new French film.*

THAT NEW FRENCH FILM, I FINISH SEE

6   *He asked Jon for $10.00.*

JON, HE (OTHER HE, NOT JON) **ASK** (MOVES TO IDENTIFY JON)
BORROW $10.00

7   *Please tell Mike to come home.*

YOU (PLEASE) TELL MIKE COME HOME

Here again we run into the use of "please" in a sentence. As stated previously this is usually shown non-manually, but can be inserted manually depending on the audience.

8   *He asked the teacher.*

TEACHER, HE FINISH ASK (MOVES TO IDENTIFY THE TEACHER)

9   *Billy pushed the girl.*

GIRL, BILLY PUSH (MOVES TO IDENTIFY GIRL)

One-directional Object Verbs

 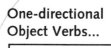

One-directional object verbs have all the characteristics of one-directional verbs, meaning they move to and identify the object of the verb. The biggest difference with these verbs is that they act on a third object within the sentence. The English equivalent of a sentence that contains this verb would be one that has a subject, object, and indirect object; for instance, "She gave the book to John." Here the subject is she, the object is book and the indirect object is John. Here is a list of the one-directional object verbs: (see right)

These verbs act similarly to travel verbs, meaning they act on an object and transport it to another location within the signing space. Therefore, they are signed in a similar fashion. Let's look at an example sentence:

One-directional Object Verbs...
Send
Give
Donate
Deliver
Bring/Carry
Buy
Pay (usually)

Example:

I sent the letter to Ohio.

CD-ROM

Here we have three objects: I, the letter, and Ohio. In this case, the verb "sent" acts on the letter and transports it to Ohio. When dealing with three objects, it is important to keep all of the spatial relationships very clear. When we look at this logically, it makes sense that we must have the object being transported by the verb in existence before we can do anything with it. Once we have done that, the sentence will flow like a travel verb sentence. The object that initiates the action will follow, and finally, the location of the transported item will be named:

LETTER, I FINISH SEND OHIO

Remember that the letter is the established topic, and the verb must move in the direction where we will place Ohio.

Example:

I gave Jane a new coat.

CD-ROM

NEW COAT, I FINISH GIVE JANE

In some instances, the object performing the action and the object being transported can be interchanged, especially when what is being transported would not make an appropriate topic. Here is an example:

Example:

Jim paid $30.00 to the doctor for a blood test.

JIM, $30.00, FINISH PAY DOCTOR FOR BLOOD TEST

Here we have Jim as the topic placed in space (on the right), $30.00 signed neutrally, PAY-TO moving towards the opposite area from where Jim was placed (to the left).

In any case, it would, however, be extremely unusual for the location object to be signed first.

It is very important in these more visually complex sentences that each piece of information is placed correctly in the signing space. Additionally, the verb's movement and direction must be carefully executed to ensure correct transmission of the concept.

As with other verbs, if any of the objects have been discussed in previous sentences and are therefore already established in the signing space, this will affect the sign order. For example, if in our previous sentence we had already introduced Jim and the doctor in our space, we would simply sign the sentence like this:

$30.00 (SIGNED IN FRONT OF BODY) HE (JIM) FINISH PAY (MOVES TOWARD DOCTOR) FOR BLOOD TEST

We don't have to re-reference the doctor because the verb itself identified the object. If we had pointed at the doctor we would have been double-indexing, as we discussed earlier. Here are a few more examples:

1   *I gave the book to Mike.*

BOOK, I FINISH GIVE MIKE

2   *Joe delivered the furniture to Helen.*

FURNITURE, JOE FINISH DELIVER HELEN

3   *Jeff bought a new car.*

NEW CAR, JEFF FINISH BUY

Here the BUY sign is literally translated as "money-give." The party to whom the money was given is not named, however it is understood to be given to someone. Therefore, the BUY sign would still move to the opposite area from Jeff, but the recipient would remain unnamed.

This concludes our discussion of verbs. By using and mastering the principles in these three chapters, you will be able to convey a conceptually accurate representation of almost anything you want to communicate. Learning how to use space correctly in establishing objects and how to correctly produce verbs are the most vital skills in signing.

9

One-directional Object Verbs

Exercises

Directions:

Rewrite the following sentences in correct ASL grammar. Practice each sentence by signing it three or four times, focusing on spatial relationships and direction of movement. If you would like to see how the sentence is signed, you can watch it on the accompanying CD-ROM.

1   I sent a letter to Spain.

2   I gave Bob a new coat.

3   Jane donated $10.00 to the United Way.

4   The man delivered the pizza late.

5   I bought a new dress at Macy's.

6   I sent the package two days ago.

7 Jim carried two crates to the warehouse.

8 I paid the phone bill yesterday.

9 I brought some cookies to the party.

9

One-directional Object Verbs

Answer Key

1 *I sent a letter to Spain.*

   LETTER, I FINISH SEND SPAIN

2 *I gave Bob a new coat.*

   NEW COAT, I FINISH GIVE BOB

3 *Jane donated $10.00 to the United Way.*

   JANE, $10.00 FINISH DONATE UNITED WAY

Here we have money being the object being transported. Rarely will a monetary amount be the topic of a sentence.

4 *The man delivered the pizza late.*

   PIZZA, MAN DELIVER LATE HE

Here, the pizza is being transported to the signer, so the sign DELIVER would move from where the man is established towards the signer's body. This entire scenario is focused on the attribute of lateness, so the whole scene is described with the LATE sign. We then must tie it all back to the originator of the action with the final HE.

5   *I bought a new dress at Macy's.*

NEW DRESS, I FINISH BUY MACY'S

In this case, we have the source of the buying being named. Therefore, the BUY (money-give) sign moves to either the right or left and Macy's is placed in the same space.

6   *I sent the package two days ago.*

TWO DAYS AGO, PACKAGE I FINISH SEND

First, we have a tense indicator to place. This is a specific tense indicator so it goes at the beginning of sentence, as discussed in Chapter 3. We then continue with the sentence as we normally would.

7   *Jim carried two crates to the warehouse.*

TWO CRATES, JIM FINISH CARRY WAREHOUSE

8   *I paid the phone bill yesterday.*

YESTERDAY, PHONE BILL I FINISH PAY

Here again we have a tense indicator to place.

9   *I brought some cookies to the party.*

COOKIES, I FINISH BRING PARTY

There are essentially two types of questions: Yes/No questions and those we will call wh questions. Yes/No questions are those that simply require a yes or no response, such as, "Have you eaten?" The Yes/No question is signed by utilizing a non-manual marker. The only difference between the signed phrase "You went to the store" and "Did you go to the store?" is this non-manual marker. The non-manual is produced throughout the entire sentence and closely resembles a topic indicator. The eyebrows are raised, the body is slightly forward, and the last sign is held for a moment longer than usual. The sign order for the yes/no sentence is determined by the normal spatial rules we have learned.

Example:

Did you go to the store?

YOU FINISH GO TO STORE (ALL WITH Y/N INDICATOR)

Wh questions are those that include the words who, what, when, where, why, how, how much, and how many. There is also a non-manual marker that accompanies this type of question. It is similar to the yes/no non-manual with one exception. The body is still slightly forward, and the last sign is held, but the eyebrows move down and together instead of up.

This non-manual is not produced throughout the entire sentence. This makes sense, since it would conflict with the topic indicator expression. Therefore, the beginning of a sentence would have a topic indicator, followed by a pause, and then a switch to the wh question non-manual.

To understand sign order in a wh question, we must first discuss What questions really are and how they are represented in our three-dimensional space. When we look at a typical question, "Who threw the ball?" what is it actually saying? If we were setting this image up in space, we see that we have a lot of information. We know that some individual threw a ball. If this sen-

103

10

tence were, "Jim threw the ball," we would:

1   *set up Jim,*

2   *give him a ball,*

3   *let him throw it.*

The problem here is that we know we have someone, we just don't know exactly who it is. Thus the wh question word itself is like a blank we are going to insert in our signing space to represent the information we lack and are therefore requesting (see next page).

This is true of all wh questions. If the sentence were, "What did you buy at the store?" we again have most of the information. We could set up the store, the person represented by "you," and the act of buying. The only piece we are missing is the item or items bought. This is where the wh question word is inserted to identify the unknown and request information about it.

We need to go into a bit more detail with topics here. Topics not only serve to anchor a sentence and identify the subject, but they also establish a point of reference for both the signer and receiver. The question-like expression of the topic indicator and the pause following the topic allow the receiver to interrupt the signer and clarify any doubts or misunderstandings. It is as if the topic indicator expression is the signer's way of checking with the receiver as each new topic is introduced, "Do you understand? Do you know what I'm talking about?" before continuing.

This is an amazing quality of ASL that assures that the signer and receiver are on the same wavelength every time a new topic is introduced. For example, if the sentence were, "That girl is my friend," and I as the receiver was not clear which girl was being referred to, I could stop the signer as soon as the topic was signed and ask for more clarification.

When we start dealing with wh questions, this clarifying role of topic indicators comes more into play. It is not only important that the simple topic be understood by both parties, but that all the information that we do know is clear before we start asking about what we don't know. That is why topics are treated a little differently in wh sentences. Usually, the entire known scenario will tend to get a topic indicator, followed by a pause and then the wh word and indicator.

Since the information we are seeking is obviously the whole point of the wh sentence, and therefore most important, the wh word will be the last sign produced in the sentence in all cases except WHO. However, some wh signs have different rules than others. There are generally four situations you will encounter with wh sentences.

What, When, Where, Why, Which, How Much, and How Many:

These are the least complex wh question sentences. Sentences with these wh question words are all signed the same way. We must remember to use all of the rules we have discussed so far, regarding use of space, verbs, and object placement. Here are a few examples:

EXAMPLE:

When are you going to the store?

> STEP 1.   YOU GO-TO STORE

This entire phrase will usually get a topic indicator. This is the known information, and thus needs to be understood by both the speaker and receiver. Thus, the clarifying role of the topic indicator comes into play. After this phrase is signed, there will be a slight pause before continuing.

> STEP 2.   WHEN (WH INDICATOR)

105

10

The wh word gets the Wh Indicator (WI)

Example:

Where is the restroom?

    Step 1.   **RESTROOM (TI)**

    Step 2.   **WHERE (WI)**

In this sentence, we have no other verb than the "to be" verb.

Example:

Which School for the Deaf did you attend?

    Step 1.   **DEAF SCHOOL (TI)**

This is the initial topic and is placed and indicated as such.

    Step 2.   **YOU GO-GO (TI)**

The known information still gets a topic indicator. The ASL phrase for "attend" is the GO sign signed twice showing the repeated action.

    Step 3.   **WHERE (WI)**

The wh word gets the wh indicator.

Example:

How much candy did you buy?

    Step 1.   **CANDY (TI)**

This sets the initial topic.

Step 2.   YOU BUY (TI)

This finishes establishing the known information.

Step 3.   HOW MUCH (WI)

This gets the wh indicator.

Example:

How many chairs did you buy?

Step 1.   CHAIRS (TI)

Sets the initial topic.

Step 2.   YOU BUY (TI)

This still gets the topic indicator since it is part of our known information.

Step 3.   HOW MANY (WI)

This gets the wh indicator.

Example:

How many people went to the concert?

Step 1.   PEOPLE (TI)

Step 2.   GO-TO CONCERT (TI)

Step 3.   HOW MANY (WI)

10

In all of these sentences when we use any of the wh words indicated, the signing order is similar.

1   *Establish initial topic with topic indicator.*

2   *Establish remainder of known information with topic indicator.*

3   *Sign the wh word at the end with the wh indicator.*

How:

"How" sentences tend to include a question phrase, not just the question word itself. The other wh words mentioned above can all stand by themselves inserted in the scene to represent the missing piece of information. However, the question "how" cannot stand alone and must be attached to a verb phrase in order to give us the exact information we need.

Example:

How do you make a chocolate cake?

Here the question involves part of the other information in the sentence, namely the verb phrase. The question we are asking is, "How do you perform a certain action?" We can't separate the question from the other phrases in the sentence, as we can with the previously mentioned wh words. This is how we would sign the sentence:

Example:

How do you make a chocolate cake?

STEP 1.   CHOCOLATE CAKE (TI)

This establishes the initial topic.

STEP 2.   YOU COOK (BAKE) HOW (WI)

This entire phrase gets the wh indicator. Remember that the wh indicator sets off the question from the rest of the sentence. Since "How do you bake" is actually the Whole question, the whole phrase will get the wh indicator.

Notice in this sentence that we had to make some sign choices for true conceptual accuracy. In English, we can say, "Make a chocolate cake," and it is clearly understood what is meant. However, the sign MAKE in ASL conveys the concept "to create", or "to manufacture." Therefore, unless the cake was made on an assembly line, or created out of nothing in a God-like fashion, the MAKE sign would be conceptually inaccurate. We have to make the switch to either COOK or BAKE.

Example:

How do you connect the printer to the computer?

CD-ROM

STEP 1.   COMPUTER, PRINTER,(TI)

This establishes the two objects in space. The computer is established as the main topic since it is considered the central object with the printer being a peripheral object.

STEP 2.   CONNECT HOW (WI)

The verb is placed with the wh word to make a wh phrase. Again, because this is actually the entire question we are asking, the entire phrase gets the wh indicator.

To summarize, when using the wh word HOW, it is generally placed with the verb in a wh phrase, the entire phrase getting the wh indicator.

109

Who:

The wh word WHO is handled a little differently. It still serves the same purpose, meaning it indicates which piece of information we don't know. The difference is that it refers to a person or people.

People are almost always the topic of the sentence, and all the other information is presented in relation to them. We said earlier that the wh word is the "blank" we insert into the scene to replace the information we don't have. In this case, the information we don't have is the topic, so the wh word will replace the topic.

People perform actions which are represented by verbs. We always have to establish who or what performed an action before the action is signed. We have also said that verbs cannot exist in space by themselves unless they are the topic of the sentence. If we don't sign WHO until the end of the sentence, and if WHO is replacing the topic, and if we can't place a verb first, then we appear to be stuck. Let's look at an example.

Example:

Jim went to the store.

JIM FINISH GO STORE.

In this sentence we place Jim first, establishing the topic, followed by the travel verb and the location. However, what if this were the sentence:

Example:

Who went to the store?

Here we have no person to place as the topic and the travel verb can't move anyone since there isn't anyone there to move.

There are two common methods to solving this problem.

Method 1: Using WHO as the topic.

In this method we insert WHO into the sentence just as if it were the person. WHO then becomes the topic of the sentence. Therefore, in the case of WHO, you will sign it at the beginning of the sentence instead of at the end.

Example:

Who went to the store?

WHO GO STORE (WI)

In cases where WHO is used as the topic, the entire sentence will get the wh indicator.

Example:

Who broke the window?

Step 1.   **WINDOW (TI)**

Here we must have the window as the topic, with the topic indicator, because it must be placed there before it can be broken.

Step 2.   **WHO BROKE (WI)**

The remaining part of the sentence gets the wh indicator.

Example:

Who brought the soda?

111

STEP 1.   SODA (TI)

STEP 2.   WHO BROUGHT (WI)

Method 2: Using classifiers to replace the topic.

In this method, we utilize the SOMEONE sign in conjunction with the person classifier that we have discussed earlier to take the place of the person who would have been the topic.

Example:

Who went to the store?

STEP 1.   SOMEONE GO-TO STORE (TI)

This places the person classifier (used in both the signs SOME-ONE and GO) into the sentence as the topic indicating an unknown person. As in our other wh sentences the entire known information receives the topic indicator.

STEP 2.   WHO THAT (REFERENCE THE AREA WHERE THE PERSON CLASSIFIER WAS PLACED) (WI)

Essentially what we are saying here is that some unknown entity went to the store. Then we ask the question, "who?" and refer to the "someone" we initially placed in the scene to ensure the question is clearly linked to the unknown person.

This method seems a little awkward, but it is more conceptually correct that Method 1. The weakness of Method 1 is that, strictly speaking, a question is an abstract idea and therefore cannot be used as a topic in a scene. Some say that using WHO in this manner is a merging of English and ASL and thus is not true ASL. These are the people who tend to use Method 2. As mentioned before, you will see both methods used among both Deaf and hearing signers.

Implied Actions:

The fourth situation you will encounter when using wh words involves actions that are implied but not actually stated. This is really a problem of translation. Because English is our first language we tend to think in English and express ourselves in ways that our language allows. When we switch to expressing our thoughts in ASL, it is important to remember that the rules are different.

This has been shown previously in the example sentences: "I want some chocolate ice cream" (where the English cultural use of "some" is different from ASL) and "How do you make a chocolate cake" (where the English word "make" is conceptually different from the ASL sign MAKE).

In the case of wh questions this comes into play when there are actions implied in a sentence but not explicitly stated.

Example:

What did you do at school?

Here we have an implied action of someone first going to school, and then doing something. This sentence assumes prior knowledge on the part of the speaker that the person was indeed going to school. This is how we would sign this sentence:

STEP 1.   **YOU FINISH GO-TO SCHOOL (TI)**

The entire first step gets a topic indicator since it is serving as a reference point for both parties and represents all known information.

STEP 2.   **DO-DO YOU (WI)**

The sign DO-DO is an ASL phrase which is equivalent to the English phrase, "What did you do?"

113

10

This type of sentence is signed similar to all other wh questions. You must set up the known scene and then insert the unknown variable to request the missing information.

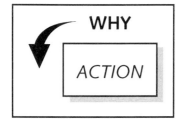

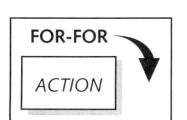

WHY vs. FOR-FOR:

One other aspect of wh questions that will be encountered is the subtle difference between the ASL signs WHY and FOR-FOR. The exclusively ASL sign FOR-FOR roughly translates into the English phrase "what for" but doesn't carry the informal aspects of the English phrase.

Sometimes in English when we ask the question "why?" we are referring to what *caused*, or *prompted* someone to perform a certain action. The ASL sign WHY is used in this circumstance. There are other times when the English "why?" is referring to the *result* or *outcome* of a certain action. In these cases the ASL sign FOR-FOR is used.

WHY:

Example:

YOU GO-TO DOCTOR WHY

"I was sick."

"I broke my arm."

The focus is on what *caused* the action to occur.

FOR-FOR:

With an ASL phrase that uses FOR-FOR, we are looking for the *result* or *outcome* of the action.

114

Example:

YOU GO-TO STORE FOR-FOR

"To get some milk."

"To get some bread."

Example:

JIM GO-TO HAWAII FOR-FOR

"To go to a wedding."

"To play golf."

All of these answers are about what was being *accomplished* by the action.

When we compare WHY and FOR-FOR, WHY is asking what happened before the action to cause the action. FOR-FOR is asking what happened after the action or what was accomplished by the action.

Look at the following English sentences and determine which would be signed as WHY and which would be signed as FOR-FOR.

1   Why is your mom so mad?

THIS WOULD BE TRANSLATED AS: **YOUR MOM MAD WHY**

This is because we are asking what caused your Mom to be angry. If we signed it with FOR-FOR it wouldn't make much sense. We would then be asking what she wanted to accomplish by being angry. Its meaning would be, "What's the point

115

of her getting so mad, it doesn't do any good?"

2 WHY DID YOUR FATHER GO TO FLORIDA?

TRANSLATION: **YOUR FATHER GO-TO FLORIDA
FOR-FOR**

Here we are looking for an answer that would tell us what he was doing in Florida, what he was accomplishing.

The difference between WHY and FOR-FOR may seem minute, but it is important in ASL. As with any langauge, there are exceptions. Sometimes WHY and FOR-FOR may be used interchangeably, but this is rare. Becoming conversant and using the language as native users do is a vital step in obtaining fluency.

NOTES

The Art of Interpreting *American Sign Language*

10

Questions

Exercise

Directions:

Rewrite each sentence using correct ASL grammar. Practice each sentence by signing it three or four times focusing on sign order and the wh indicator. If you would like to see how the sentence is signed, you can watch it on the accompanying CD-ROM.

1   *Who broke the window?*

2   *What did you buy at the store?*

3   *When does the meeting start?*

4   *Where are my keys?*

5   *Why was your boss so mad?*

6   *How do you make french toast?*

7   *How much did that book cost?*

8   *How many people attended the wedding?*

9   *Which do you prefer, coffee or tea?*

10

Questions

Answer Key

1   *Who broke the window?*

   WINDOW (TI) WHO BROKE (WI)

Here we have to establish the window as the topic followed by the remaining part of the sentence with the wh indicator.

2   *What did you buy at the store?*

   STEP 1.   YOU FINISH GO-TO STORE (TI)

   STEP 2.   BUY WHAT (WI)

This is a sentence with an implied action. We have to get the person to the store, and then have the person buy something.

3   *When is the meeting?*

   MEETING (TI) TIME WHAT (WI)

4   *Where are my keys?*

   MY KEYS (TI) WHERE (WI)

5   *Why was your boss so mad?*

   YOUR BOSS MAD (TI) WHY (WI)

6 *How do you make french toast?*

FRENCH TOAST (TI) COOK HOW (WI)

Here we have to change "make" to COOK as in our previous example.

7 *How much did that book cost?*

BOOK THAT (TI) COST HOW-MUCH (WI)

8 *How many people attended the wedding?*

PEOPLE ATTEND WEDDING (TI) HOW-MANY (WI)

9 *Which do you prefer, coffee or tea?*

COFFEE (TI) TEA (TI) YOU PREFER WHICH (WI)

N e g a t i o n

Negatives are words or signs that act to nullify the effect of other words or signs within a sentence. In English, the words that perform this function are words such as not, can't, won't, don't, etc. Negatives act very similar to wh sentences within a three-dimensional signing space. To see this we must examine what negation does. Here is a typical English sentence with a negative:

Example:

I didn't go to work.

In this sentence, we are told of an event that didn't happen. This is an unusual function in language. To understand this mentally, we must visualize the person actually performing the action or event and then somehow mentally tag it as "not happening."

Because ASL mirrors our actual thought process, this is the same way that negation will be used in our signing space. We will state the positive scenario and then negate it. Here is a list of negative signs in ASL: (see right).

Before we continue in our discussion of negation, we need to define each of the above signs. Just as with WHY and FOR-FOR, some of these signs carry different or more restricted meanings in ASL than they do in English.

Negation Signs...

> Not
> Can't
> Won't
> Don't
> Never
> Nothing
> Not-Yet
> No

NOT:

This is the universal negation. It's most similar to the English prefix "un-" and is the only negation which you will consistently see before a verb.

Example:

That is not an ostrich.

CAN'T:

This means to not have the ability or permission to do something. It is similar to its English equivalent.

Example:

I can't go to your party.

WON'T:

This means to willfully choose not to do something, or to refuse. This is not, however, always equivalent to the English.

Example:

I won't clean my room.

My T.V. won't work

These are both correct in English. But in ASL the second sentence would not use the WON'T sign. In this example, unless your T.V. is marching around the living room with a picket sign, the WON'T sign would not be appropriate.

DON'T:

This sign is always outwardly directed, i.e. "don't-you." It is used as a warning or command. It would never be used in reference to oneself. Because of this, it is rarely used in ASL.

Example:

Don't play with matches.

Don't see that movie.

It would not be correct to use this sign as it is in these English sentences:

I don't drink.

I don't have any money.

NEVER:

This is the exact equivalent to the English usage.

Example:

I've never been to Greece.

NOTHING (NO, NONE):

This is a sign of quantity. It shows the lack of something.

Example:

I have no money.

NOT-YET:

This sign is similar to its English equivalent. It is used in place of the English words: haven't, hasn't, has not, or have not.

Example:

I haven't eaten.

NO:

This means the opposite of Yes. We must be careful not to confuse it with the quantity sign for nothing.

Example:

No, thank you.

It would not be correct to use this sign in the sentence:

I have no money.

Now that we have clarified the meanings of the different negative signs, let's look at them grammatically. As we said before, negation acts on an action or an event that is already visualized. Therefore, the rule with negatives is that they will follow the word or concept they negate. We will first establish the scene or action and then negate it. They will most commonly appear at the end of the sentence.

The non-manual marker which accompanies these negatives is a shaking of the head and a natural negative expression on the face. This Negation Indicator (NI) usually only appears on the negating sign itself or during the verb phrase. The rest of the sentence will get a topic indicator and other indicators as appropriate. This occurs because the topic indicator and the negation indicator are opposite expressions (see left).

Example:

CD-ROM

Bob can't read.

BOB READ (TI), CAN'T (NI) HE (RE-INDEXING BOB)

We establish Bob as the topic and place him, we then retain the topic indicator as we sign the verb READ, and finally we negate the entire scene with the CAN'T sign and the negation indicator.

Example:

Jim can't go to the movies.

STEP 1. JIM (TI)

STEP 2. GO-TO MOVIE (TI)

STEP 3. CAN'T (NI)

STEP 4. HE (RE-INDEXING JIM WITH THE NI CONTINUING)

Notice that in both of these sentences, whether we are negating a simple verb (READ) or an entire verb phrase (GO-TO MOVIES), the topic indicator is still held throughout the entire phrase. There will also be a pause between the initial topic and the verb phrase, and the verb phrase and the negative.

Remember that with this use of negation we are actually signing the positive sentence and then negating it. Negation is not only shown by the negative itself, but also by how we re-index the topic. Remember we said that one-directional travel verbs transport the topic to another location. In negation sentences, when you re-index the topic, you do so back in the original position, not in the location they would be in if they had actually performed the action.

Other negative signs have "built-in" negation. The sign is modified to show it is now a negative. Here is a list of these built-in negation signs: (see right).

Each of these signs in the left column can be modified in its execution to become negative.

Negation Signs...	
Like	Don't Like
Want	Don't Want
Know	Don't Know
Good	Bad

Example:

Sue doesn't want to go to bed.

STEP 1. SUE (TI)

STEP 2.   GO-TO BED (TI)

STEP 3.   DOESN'T WANT (NI) SHE

We still sign the sentence the same way, with the built in negation at the end.

Example:

I don't like onions.

STEP 1.   ONIONS (TI)

STEP 2.   DON'T LIKE I (NI)

A negation sentence with the subject "I" is often signed as above, with the "I" at the end. As we said before, it is unusual for "I" to be the topic of a sentence. However, if it is important to stress the subject, this sentence could be signed:

I ONIONS (TI) DON'T LIKE (NI)

There are a few other principles that will help when using negation. This pattern of the negative appearing after the word or concept it negates is true of all negatives except for NOT. As we stated earlier, NOT is very similar to the English prefix "un-" and acts in the same way to automatically negate the sign it is attached to. Because of this you will often see NOT before the verb and actually incorporated into the sign.

Example:

I didn't go to the movies.

This could be signed in two ways:

1. I NOT GO-TO MOVIES (ALL NI)

2.   MOVIES (TI), I GO-TO (TI), NOT (NI)

The first method is more common; the second method places special emphasis on the negation. If the negative were unusually stressed, the NOT would appear both before and after the verb:

Example:

I NOT GO-TO MOVIES NOT (ALL NI)

Finally, any action or event can be negated simply by shaking the head throughout the sentence with no actual negative sign being included. In this case, the topic still receives a topic indicator, and the rest of the sentence gets a negation indicator. This is most often used in a casual environment and would not be seen in a business or formal setting.

Example:

Jim didn't go to the meeting.

JIM (TI), GO-TO MEETING (ALL SIGNED WITH HEAD SHAKE)

11

Negation

Exercises

Directions:

Rewrite each sentence in correct ASL grammar. Practice each sentence three or four times signing it with focus on the negation indicator and correct sign order. If you would like to see how the sentence is signed, you can watch it on the accompanying CD-ROM.

1   I can't go to the movies.

2   Betty doesn't want to clean her room.

3   Alicia doesn't have a dress for the dance

4   Please don't play with the remote control!

5   I will never to go an opera.

6   I have no money!

7   *Jeff hasn't paid his phone bill.*

8   *I can't sign well.*

9   *Mike really doesn't like milk.*

The Art of Interpreting *American Sign Language*

Negation

Answer Key

1   *I can't go to the movies.*

   I GO-TO MOVIES (TI) CAN'T I (NI)

2   *Betty doesn't want to clean her room.*

   STEP 1.   **BETTY (TI)**

   STEP 2.   **CLEAN ROOM (TI)**

   STEP 3.   **DOESN'T WANT SHE (NI)**

3   *Alicia doesn't have a dress for the dance.*

   STEP 1.   **ALICIA (TI)**

   STEP 2.   **DRESS HAVE FOR DANCE (TI)**

   STEP 3.   **NOT (NI) SHE**

4   *Please don't play with the remote control!*

   STEP 1.   **YOU "PLAY-WITH-REMOTE-CONTROL" (TI)**

   STEP 2.   **DON'T(NI)**

The understood subject "you" would have to be inserted. Also, the act of playing with the remote control would have to be mimed. You could not sign it literally because the sign PLAY means to use as a toy and does not translate into the English well in this sentence. You could also sign BOTHER the remote control. Another way to sign this sentence would be if a child was in the act of playing with the remote control. If you wanted them to stop immediately, you would sign:

STEP 2.   FINISH (NI)

This is how you say "Stop it!" in ASL.

5   *I will never to go an Australia.*

STEP 1.   AUSTRALIA (TI)

STEP 2.   I GO-TO WILL (TI)

STEP 3.   NEVER (NI)

In this sentence it is important to include the sign WILL in the negated portion of the sentence (everything before the negation sign). In this case WILL is not a tense indicator but is part of the negated concept, and therefore will appear before the negative.

6   *I have no money!*

I HAVE MONEY NONE (ALL NI)

7   *Jeff hasn't paid his phone bill.*

STEP 1.   PHONE BILL (TI)

Step 2.   **JEFF PAY (TI)**

Step 3.   **NOT-YET HE (NI)**

This sentence includes a one-directional object verb so either JEFF or PHONE BILL can be the topic.

8   *I can't sign well.*

I SIGN WELL (TI) CAN'T I (NI)

Here it is important to include WELL before the negative since it is also part of what is being negated.

9   *Mike really doesn't like milk.*

Step 1.   **MILK (TI)**

Step 2.   **MIKE (TI)**

Step 3.   **DOESN'T LIKE ++ (NI)**

In this sentence, as mentioned earlier, the word "really" is usually not signed but is produced non-manually. The negative expression is increased as well as the speed and size of the sign DOESN'T LIKE. This is the same in sentences which use true, truly, very, extremely, etc.

Conditional sentences are what we express in English as if/then sentences.

Example:

If you don't go to school, then you won't graduate.

These are compound sentences in which the second phrase is caused by the first phrase. Grammatically we treat these as two completely separate scenes, joined by a transitional sign or non-manually which establishes a causal relationship.

In conditional sentences we are dealing with twice the information we would normally sign. Therefore, it is important to keep all of the information carefully placed and integrated within the signing space. There are very clear rules governing conditional sentences.

1   **The first sign that always appears is the
    SUPPOSE sign.**

This sign is produced even before any tense indicators or other signs that we have learned are usually signed at the beginning of sentences.

2   **The entire first phrase of the conditional sentence
    gets a topic indicator.**

3   **The first phrase is all signed on one side of the body,
    followed by a pause.**

4   **The transitional sign is signed in the center of the body, fol-
    lowed by a pause. This sign is usually MEAN or MAYBE.**

12

The transitional sign used is determined by the relationship between the first and second phrase. If the second phrase is *absolutely* caused by the first, then you use MEAN. If the second phrase *might* be caused by the first phrase, MAYBE is used.

Either one of these (MEAN or MAYBE) can be produced non-manually as well, during a pause between the first and second phrases. An emphatic head-nod would equate to the sign MEAN. A slight shoulder shrug with a slight side-to-side bobbing of the head would equate to the sign MAYBE.

5   The second phrase of the sentence is signed on the opposite side of the signing space as the first phrase. The second phrase is also accompanied by a head-nod for positive phrases or the negation indicator for a negative phrase. The only time this would not be true is if the object is the same in both phrases.

Example:

If Jane has ice cream, I am going to her house.

During the first phrase we set up Jane and the ice cream all on one side of the signing space. When we sign the second phrase, we have to put Jane's house in the same space as Jane. Additionally, the verb GO moves towards Jane. Therefore, because the objects are all associated in one space for both phrases, we can't sign the second phrase on the opposite side of the signing space.

One other factor that affects conditional sentences is the effect of grammatical rules on the second phrase. These sentences, because they contain two phrases, usually are much longer than a typical ASL phrase. As more information is presented from the beginning of the first phrase until the end, more misunderstandings can occur. Therefore, grammatical rules which interfere

136

with the steady flow of information will tend to be overlooked. For example, if the second phrase has multiple objects, the topic indicator pause is extremely short, or even omitted, to keep the sentence flowing.

Example:

If it snows tomorrow, school will be canceled.

STEP 1.   SUPPOSE TOMORROW SNOW (TI) (ALL SIGNED RIGHT)

STEP 2.   MEAN (SIGNED CENTER)

STEP 3.   SCHOOL CANCEL WILL (ALL SIGNED LEFT WIT HEAD-NOD)

Example:

If the car breaks down, we will have to walk to the gas station.

STEP 1.   SUPPOSE CAR BREAK-DOWN (TI) (ALL RIGHT)

STEP 2.   MEAN (SIGNED CENTER)

STEP 3.   WE WALK-TO GAS STATION MUST I (ALL LEFT WITH HEAD NOD)

These sentences may appear to be complicated, but we must look at them three-dimensionally. We have the first part of the sentence describing a scene that may occur. Then we are saying that if the first phrase actually happens it means that this entire event, placed on the other side of the body, will also occur. Here are some more examples.

Example:

If you don't clean your room, you can't go to the movies.

STEP 1. **SUPPOSE YOU CLEAN YOUR ROOM NOT (TI) (RIGHT)**

STEP 2. **YOU GO MOVIES CAN'T YOU (ALL NI) (LEFT)**

Here we transition with just an extended pause. Also note in step 1, the negation NOT still gets a topic indicator, not a negation indicator. This will be true in all cases.

Example:

If John gets sick, who's going to pitch for the game?

STEP 1. **SUPPOSE JOHN SICK (TI) (RIGHT)**

STEP 2. **WHO PITCH GAME (WI)**

Example:

Because it rained yesterday, the game will be canceled today.

STEP 1. **YESTERDAY RAIN (TI) (RIGHT)**

STEP 2. **MEANS (CENTER)**

STEP 3. **TODAY, GAME CANCEL (LEFT WITH HEAD NOD)**

Here we have a case where the event in the first half of the sentence has already occurred. This causes the SUPPOSE sign to be omitted. However, the sentence is still treated exactly like a conditional sentence. Here is another example of this.

Example:

I bought a ticket, but I can't go.

STEP 1.   TICKET I FINISH BUY (TI) (RIGHT)

STEP 2.   BUT (CENTER)

STEP 3.   I GO CAN'T (NI) (LEFT)

Rhetorical Questions:

Sometimes the two halves of the sentence are reversed chronologically, as in, "The game was canceled because it rained." The rain actually happened before the cancellation. This is usually done to emphasize the cause instead of the effect.

This can be done in ASL as well. In ASL, we know if we want to emphasize something, we move it to the end of the sentence. However, because we will be breaking the rule of chronological order, we must use a special technique called the rhetorical question.

A rhetorical question is one that the speaker does not expect an answer to; it is asked for some other effect. The rhetorical question in ASL is most often used in cases where the action in the first half of the sentence has already taken place, therefore, the SUPPOSE sign will not be used. When using the rhetorical question to reverse the chronological order of events, a wh word is used in place of the transitional sign between the two phrases.

When doing this, the non-manual changes from a wh indicator to a Rhetorical Question Indicator (RI). This indicator is very similar to the expression used for a topic indicator. The eyebrows are up. However, the body stays back and the pause is much

12

shorter. This shows that you are not expecting an answer from the receiver of the message, but are going to supply the answer yourself.

Example:

I got mad because by brother read my diary.

STEP 1.   I MAD (TI, LEFT)

STEP 2.   WHY (RI, CENTER)

STEP 3.   MY   BROTHER   (TI)   READ   MY   D-I-A-R-Y (ALL LEFT)

Example:

I went to the store because I ran out of milk.

STEP 1.   I GO-TO STORE (TI, RIGHT)

STEP 2.   WHY (RI, CENTER)

STEP 3.   MILK RUN-OUT ME (ALL LEFT)

Example:

The game was canceled because of the rain.

STEP 1.   GAME CANCEL (TI, RIGHT)

STEP 2.   WHY (RI, CENTER)

STEP 3.   RAIN (LEFT)

NOTES

The Art of Interpreting *American Sign Language*

12

Conditionals

Exercises

Directions:

Rewrite each sentence using correct ASL grammar. Practice each sentence three or four times focusing on signing each phrase with the transition in the appropriate space. If you would like to see how the sentence is signed, you can watch it on the accompanying CD-ROM.

1   *If the plane is delayed, I will be mad.*

2   *If you give me the money, I'll buy the ticket.*

3   *If I buy the tickets, I'll let you know.*

4   *If you're going to Chicago, I'll go with you.*

5   *If Jim has a VCR, I'll go to his house.*

6   *If he wants to learn ASL, he will have to practice.*

7   *I can't go to Florida because my aunt is visiting.*

8   *If it rains tomorrow, the concert will be canceled.*

9   *If you want to go to the movies, you have to clean your room.*

143

Conditionals

Answer Key

1   *If the plane is delayed, I will be mad.*

    STEP 1.   **SUPPOSE PLANE DELAY (TI, LEFT)**

    STEP 2.   **I MAD WILL I (RIGHT WITH HEAD-NOD)**

2   *If you give me the money, I'll buy the ticket.*

    STEP 1.   **SUPPOSE MONEY YOU-GIVE-ME (TI, LEFT)**

    STEP 2.   **MEAN (CENTER)**

    STEP 3.   **I BUY TICKET WILL I**

Here we see the decreasing effect of the grammatical rules on the second phrase. Normally we would have to sign TICKET before the object verb, but because this would interrupt the flow of the sentence, it is signed as shown above.

3   *If I buy the tickets, I'll let you know.*

    STEP 1.   **SUPPOSE TICKETS I BUY (TI, LEFT)**

    STEP 2.   **I LET-YOU-KNOW WILL I (RIGHT WITH HEAD NOD)**

4   *If you're going to Chicago, I'll go with you.*

    STEP 1.   **SUPPOSE YOU GO-TO CHICAGO (TI, RIGHT)**

STEP 2.   **I GO-WITH WILL I** (ALSO RIGHT WITH HEAD NOD)

Here both phrases are signed on the same side of the signing space because GO-WITH and GO-TO both refer to CHICAGO.

5   *If Jim has a VCR, I'll go to his house.*

    STEP 1.   **SUPPOSE JIM VCR HAVE** (TI, RIGHT)

    STEP 2.   **MEAN** (CENTER)

    STEP 3.   **I GO HIS HOUSE WILL I** (ALSO RIGHT WITH HEAD NOD)

6   *If he wants to learn ASL, he will have to practice.*

    STEP 1.   **SUPPOSE HE ASL LEARN WANT** (TI LEFT)

    STEP 2.   **MEAN** (CENTER)

    STEP 3.   **PRACTICE MUST HE** (RIGHT WITH HEAD NOD)

Here the signs PRACTICE and MUST will appear on the right, while the HE will be indexed back on the left.

7   *I can't go to Florida because my aunt is visiting.*

    STEP 1.   **I GO FLORIDA CAN'T** (NI, LEFT)

    STEP 2.   **WHY** (RI, CENTER)

    STEP 3.   **MY AUNT VISIT** (RIGHT WITH HEAD NOD)

The Art of Interpreting *American Sign Language*

8   *If it rains tomorrow, the trip to the zoo will be canceled.*

    STEP 1.   **SUPPOSE TOMORROW RAIN (TI, LEFT)**

    STEP 2.   **MEAN (CENTER)**

    STEP 3.   **GROUP-GO ZOO CANCEL WILL (RIGHT WITH HEAD NOD)**

9   *If you want to go to the movies, you have to clean your room.*

    STEP 1.   **SUPPOSE YOU GO-TO MOVIE WANT (TI, RIGHT)**

    STEP 2.   **MEAN (CENTER)**

    STEP 3.   **YOU CLEAN ROOM MUST YOU (LEFT WITH HEAD NOD)**

Direct Discourse and Role Taking

We have discussed the use of space to relate concepts and objects to each other. We have established relationships by placing objects in space, relaying information about these objects, or relating objects and concepts to each other through the manipulation of space. We are now going to move into the true essence and beauty of ASL.

ASL, because of its visual, three-dimensional quality, can actually replay events using the space in front of the signer. Instead of simply describing events to an audience, we can actually take them there "real time." In English, we relate events in this manner: "Yesterday I went to the store." In ASL, we are transported back in time to yesterday and re-live the event. This is one of the most incredible qualities of ASL, and one that few non-native signers ever master. This presents difficulty for the interpreter, who must relay someone else's experiences as if they were his own. Interpreters have to glean a lot of information from the context, voice intonation, and expression of the speaker or signer to relay an accurate account of the experience.

Signers who are relaying events which they have actually experienced have a less difficult time because they have a detailed recollection of the event to draw upon. However, in both of these cases, relaying events in ASL can be difficult if too much English influence creeps in.

One rule to remember when relaying events is called the "Show, don't tell" rule. The easiest way to understand this principle is by first discussing the role of conversations or direct discourse, and how they function in English and in ASL. In English, relaying a conversation we have previsouly had usually looks something like this: "Jane told me to go home."

In ASL, we transport our audience back in time to the actual conversation. We take on the persona or role of Jane, and show much more than a simple description can tell in the same amount of time. This is what we mean by role taking. Role taking in ASL means to sign a concept by taking on the role of a character you have placed in front of you, so that everything you sign or do is assumed to be the words or actions of the person placed in space.

13

We will start demonstrating this principle with the easiest situation to understand, a direct discourse dialogue. The English sentence is, "Jane told me to go home." The sentence is past tense, but if I am relating a previous event to you, it is obvious that it must have happened in the past. Unless there is a specific time indicator, all actions are assumed past tense, so you don't have to worry about the past tense of the verb "told." Let's look at the steps in role taking.

Step 1:

First we must set up the main characters. The "I" is the signer, so we only need to worry about Jane. We place Jane in space by spelling her name, and/or giving her name sign, and then pointing to the left or right. We will choose left for this example. So now, in my signing space, I am standing in the middle and Jane in assumed to be standing on my left.

We then set up the beginning of the dialogue, or signal that a conversation took place. We do this by using the sign TELL-ME. This is a one-directional sign, therefore we will start the sign to our left where Jane is and move it towards us. As soon as the sign TELL-ME ends, we then take on the role of Jane. We do this by shifting our shoulders to the left, and looking to the right. We move our torso a little bit back, so it seems as if we are actually moving into Jane's space. This movement is very small and is mainly done with the torso, head, and eye gaze. Many interpreters and signers make the mistake of exaggerating these movements or actually moving their feet to take on a role. The correct movement is very small and controlled.

If Jane is on our left, and looking at us, then we are obviously on her right. That is why when we take her role, we look to the right as if we were Jane looking at us. At this point we have become Jane, and anything we say or do will be assumed to be Jane's words or actions.

One thing that is vital here is that as long as we are in the role of Jane, we must not look at the receiver of our message.

Remember that we have gone back in time to when the actual event took place. The person to whom we are relating this event probably wasn't there. If we look at that person, it disrupts the role taking process.

Step 2:

Now that we have shoulder-shifted, and are looking to the right, we have become Jane. We simply have to say what Jane said, "Go home." We say it in the same manner as we perceived Jane to have said it. It is very important to convey the spirit of what Jane said. The mannerisms and body language are as much a part of the message as the words themselves.

Step 3:

After we complete the phrase, we go back to the neutral position and shift our eye gaze back to the receiver. This signals that we have returned from the past and the role taking is over. Let's look at some more examples.

> *Example: I told him I couldn't go to the party.*

STEP 1:   I TELL-TO

This sign is directional from the center of the body to the left where we assume we have previously established "him" in our sentence. This sets us up for the role take. As we finish the sign TELL-TO we also shift the shoulders, face to the right, and eye gaze left where "him" is located. This takes us back in time to the original conversation.

STEP 2.   I GO-TO PARTY CAN'T I

This acts out to the receiver of our message the exact words, expression, and feeling of what was said. It is more descriptive than simply relaying the words. For example, I could be disappointed or angry about not being able to go. This would show in my signs and expressions.

STEP 3. SHOULDER SHIFT BACK TO NEUTRAL POSITION AND EYE GAZE THE RECEIVER.

This takes me out of the role take and back to the present.

This is the basic mechanism for all direct discourse situations and ASL role taking in general. Role taking is one of the most highly used and most effective tools in ASL. It is used in every register from intimate to rigid and is how the vast majority of events are relayed in ASL.

There are a few more things we have to take into account with role taking. In ASL, relationships are very important. Not only spatial relationships, but relationships between people as well. There are generally three kinds of relationships between people in ASL: superior to subordinate, equal to equal, and subordinate to superior. These relationships are defined by several different characteristics, such as age, social standing, and authority.

For example, if a child is talking to a parent, teacher, or older individual, he would be in a subordinate to superior relationship. Also, if a normal citizen were talking to a policeman, supervisor, or famous person, this too would be portrayed as a subordinate to superior relationship.

However, there are also other characteristics that are simply situational. For example, suppose Jim had done something to offend Jane and was apologizing. Within that situation, regardless of age, social standing, or authority, Jim would be portrayed as a subordinate speaking to a superior. Other situations where this would take place would be if someone were borrowing something, asking for a favor, or trying to flatter someone. All of these would put the person in the subordinate category.

As I said before, these relationships are very important and will govern how role taking is done to represent the people in these roles. The two main things that these relationships affect in terms of role taking are eye gaze and vocabulary choice.

When in a role take between a subordinate and a superior, the subordinate will eye gaze not only in the direction of the superior, but will also look slightly up, and the superior eye gaze will be slightly down. This is true regardless of the actual physical location of either party. The higher the eye gaze, the more important the person is; the lower the eye gaze the more unimportant the person, comparatively speaking.

Vocabulary choice and style of signing are also affected by these relationships. There are some signs you simply don't use when talking to a superior. As in English, subtle variances in word choice must be considered. Let's look at the sign TELL. You can TELL an equal and you can TELL a subordinate. But you never TELL a superior unless you were being cocky or sassy. You INFORM a superior.

A superior can INFORM subordinates, but it would be interpreted as showing humility and gracious inclusiveness, not admitting to a lesser standing. Similarly, when addressing a superior, the signing style is smaller and more "humble." The signs are brought in closer to the body and do not move quickly or angrily. If we move quickly and angrily when talking to a superior in a role take, the eye gaze would still be upward. What we would be communicating is that we went beyond the cultural norm and were causing trouble or were "facing down" a bad authority figure. As you can see, these relationships can tremendously affect our role taking, and therefore must be accurately deduced and portrayed.

Example:

The judge told me I had to pay a fine of $50.00.

In this example, we are obviously the subordinate, therefore our eye gaze would be upward whenever we are "us" and downward whenever we are the judge. Also the physical conditions of the situation require us to look up at the judge seated on his dais.

13

STEP 1. JUDGE (TI) TELL-ME

If we have placed the judge on the left, the TELL-ME sign would move from the left towards us. As the TELL sign finishes, we shoulder-shift left and eye gaze downward to the right. We take on the affect of the judge (back held straight, face stern).

STEP 2. YOU, PAY $50.00 FINE MUST YOU

This is all signed in the affect of the judge, relaying both the exact words and feelings of the judge as interpreted by the signer.

STEP 3. DROP AFFECT OF JUDGE. SHOULDER-SHIFT BACK TO NEUTRAL, EYE GAZE BACK TO RECEIVER.

This takes us out of the role and back to the present.

Another situation we encounter is when there is a reply to the first sentence. All of the same rules apply, but now we must take on the role of the other person in the conversation and reply.

Example:

I told my mom we were out of milk and she told me to go to the store to buy some.

STEP 1. MY MOTHER (TI) I TELL-TO

At then end of the TELL sign, shift shoulders to left (assuming MOTHER is on the right) shift eye gaze upwards to indicate superior relationship.

STEP 2. MILK (TI) RUN-OUT

This is signed in the affect of "I." At the end of this phrase, shoulder shift to right, assume eye gaze and affect of MOTHER.

Step 3.   YOU GO-TO STORE (TI), BUY

This phrase is signed in the affect of the MOTHER. At the end of the phrase, shoulder-shift back to neutral position and eye gaze receiver, indicating end of role take.

Now that we have talked about direct discourse, let's move on to relating other events. This is often called story telling. When we relate or interpret a series of events that have enough detail to act out, we should do so in a role take. Here is an example:

Example:

> I was driving home yesterday when some guy cut
> me off at the toll booth. I was furious! I honked
> at him and said, "What's the matter with you!"
> It really bothered me.

This monologue provides us with sufficiently detailed information to recreate the scene through a role take. While relating events such as this you use a technique called zoom in/zoom out. You zoom in to a scene to take on a role and show direct dialogue or actions performed by a person in the scene, and then you zoom out as a narrator to set up a scene or move pieces around in the scene.

The first step in signing this particular scene would be to set up the general background. This would be with you in a car driving along the highway. This is what you must set up first.

Step 1. (zoom out) YESTERDAY, I DRIVE-TO HOME

Step 2. (zoom in)   Drop eye gaze as if in a car driving, looking out the windshield, affect neutral.

Step 3. (zoom out) Eye gaze back to the receiver, indicating you are now narrating new information.

TOLL NEAR, SOMEONE (Using the vehicle classifier, show a car pull up from behind and quickly pull in front of your car.)

>STEP 4. (ZOOM IN) EYE GAZE THE CAR IN FRONT OF YOU, INDICATING YOU ARE BACK IN THE ROLE TAKE. AFFECT IS ANGRY AND SHOCKED. ACT OUT HONKING THE HORN. RAISE HAND IN QUESTIONING MANNER. SHOW THE ANGER, DON'T TELL THE ANGER THROUGH ANY SIGNS.

>STEP 5. (ZOOM OUT) RETURN EYE GAZE TO RECEIVER.

>**TRUE UPSET ME**

This indicates narrated information, ends the role take, and allows the receiver to comment on the scene.

Other factors that need to be considered in relaying events are:

1   Whenever a specific time indicator is not provided to indicate exactly when an event occured, a general introductory time indicator must be provided. These are usually the signs: HAPPEN, ONE DAY, or ONE TIME.

2   Any time a new object or person is introduced into the setting, you must zoom out, name the object and place it in the scene. You may then zoom back in the role take and interact with that object or person.

The key concept in relaying events through role taking, or story telling, is that you show the actions you don't tell the actions. For example, if someone said, "The boy looked up and smiled at me," you wouldn't sign that word for word. Instead, you would introduce the boy, take on his role, and act out the looking up and smiling.

This concept of entering and exiting roles is an integral part of ASL. Mastering this skill will move a signer or interpreter from adequate to excellent. It is the heart of ASL.

NOTES

Direct Discourse and Role Taking

Exercises

Directions:

Rewrite each sentence using correct ASL grammar. Practice each sentence three or four times focusing on signing each phrase with the transition in the appropriate space. If you would like to see how the sentence is signed, you can watch it on the accompanying CD-ROM.

1   I told her she couldn't borrow my dress.

2   The policeman told me I was driving too fast.

3   My mother called to tell me about her new apartment.

4   The teacher told me I need to pay attention in class.

5   Last week I was turning left at a light when some moron plowed into the back of me.

6   The coach told the player he was off the team.

7   I went to the ice machine and realized I left my key back in the room.

8   I was watching T.V. when suddenly the lights went out.

9   I was driving down the road when I saw a woman whose car had broken down, so I decided to stop and help.

Direct Discourse and Role Taking

Answer Key

1   I told her she couldn't borrow my dress.

> **STEP 1.**   I TELL-TO HER
>
> **STEP 2.**   (SHIFT, SUPERIOR ROLE TAKE) YOU BORROW MY DRESS CAN'T

2   The policeman told me I was driving too fast.

> **STEP 1.**   POLICEMAN (TI) TELL-ME
>
> **STEP 2.**   (SUPERIOR ROLE TAKE) YOU DRIVE TOO FAST

3   My mother called to tell me about her new apartment.

> **STEP 1.**   MY MOTHER CALL ME
>
> **STEP 2.**   SHE TELL-ME ABOUT NEW APARTMENT

This sentence is not actually a direct discourse. There is nothing we can quote from the mother. Therefore, it is relayed as shown above.

4   The teacher told me I need to pay attention in class.

> **STEP 1.**   TEACHER (TI) SHE TELL-ME
>
> **STEP 2.**   (SUPERIOR ROLE TAKE
> YOU PAY ATTENTION

5   *Last week I was turning left at a light when some moron plowed into the back of me.*

     Step 1. (zoom out) **LAST WEEK, I DRIVING.**

     Step 2. (zoom in)   Show driving casually.

     Step 3. (zoom out) **LIGHT (TI) I** (show vehicle classifier beginning to make a left turn) **HAPPEN** (show second vehicle classifier behind car turning left running into back of first car)

     Step 4. (zoom in) While the "accident" is occurring take on the affect of being hit from behind and the reaction. **MORON YOU.**

     Step 5. (zoom out) Return to neutral position, eye gaze receiver

6   *The official told the player he was out of the game.*

     Step 1.   **OFFICIAL (TI) TELL-TO PLAYER (TI)**

     Step 2.   (superior role take) **YOU OUT.**

7   *I went to the ice machine and realized I left my key back in the room.*

     Step 1.(zoom out) **I HOTEL(TI)**

This sentence has to be used to introduce the scene if it hasn't been established already.

I GO FOR ICE

STEP 2.(ZOOM IN) WITH THE PERSON CLASSIFIER, SHOW SOMEONE WALKING DOWN THE HALL. **A**T THE SAME TIME TAKE ON THE AFFECT AND EYE GAZE AS IF YOU WERE WALKING DOWN THE HALL, PROBABLY HOLDING AN ICE BUCKET.

I REALIZE MY KEY THERE ROOM LEFT (POINT BACK BEHIND TO WHERE THE ROOM IS)

8   *I was watching T.V. when suddenly the lights went out.*

STEP 1. (ZOOM OUT) **ONE TIME I WATCH T.V.**

STEP 2. (ZOOM IN) TAKE ON AFFECT AND EYE GAZE OF WATCHING **T.V.**

STEP 3. (ZOOM OUT) **HAPPEN LIGHTS OFF**

STEP 4. (ZOOM IN) TAKE ON AFFECT OF SURPRISE.

STEP 5 (ZOOM OUT) RETURN TO NEUTRAL POSITION AND EYE GAZE

9   *I was driving down the road when I saw a woman whose car had broken down, so I decided to stop and help.*

STEP 1. (ZOOM OUT) **ONE TIME I DRIVE**

STEP 2. (ZOOM IN) TAKE ON AFFECT OF DRIVING

STEP 3. (ZOOM OUT) **I SPOT WOMAN (TI) PARK** SHOW VEHICLE CLASSIFIER PARKED ON SIDE OF ROAD

STEP 4. (ZOOM IN) EYE GAZE **WOMAN**, CONCERNED/CURIOUS AFFECT

STEP 5. (ZOOM OUT) **HER CAR BROKE DOWN**

STEP 6. (ZOOM IN) I STOP HELP

This sentence can be done in the role take almost as if talking to yourself, or it can be done out of the role take as narration.

Conclusion

As we come to the end of this book, which is the first in a planned three-part series, I feel it is important to look back at what we have accomplished. We began with a discussion of language as a means to communicate concepts, and these concepts or pictures within our minds are the basis for all communication. The closer we come to accurately conveying these mental images, the more accurate our communication will be. We have looked at ASL as a visual three dimensional language capable of more closely mirroring these concepts than any other language. With ASL we take objects out of the mental, conceptual realm and actually reproduce them in space. We assign attributes to these concepts and have them interact in our signing space, recreating events and portraying feelings.

The previous chapters have taken you through some of the rules involved in this amazing process. However, as we analyze ASL step by step, we often lose sight of the magic that it contains when all the rules work together to create a whole. I have learned several languages, but none that I have ever encountered have the power to communicate like ASL. Incredible levels of nuance, meaning and emotion can be portrayed through a turn of the wrist, the shift of a gaze and the slightest of expressions.

Therefore, I encourage you to study and master the basic building blocks of ASL that this book contains which is your first step in becoming fluent, and begin to glimpse this magic within ASL. If your aim is to move on and become an interpreter, you have elected to enter one of the greatest professions available to you. Interpreters have the unique opportunity to grasp communication within their hands and to become a tool of interaction between people. In doing so we glimpse a small part of almost every profession and every walk of life. We provide an amazing service on stage in front of hundreds, or in quiet back rooms; in situations of joy and celebration, or sometimes sadness and loss.

We are almost never recognized except when we make a mistake, but that is why we are here, to provide a transparent window between worlds of communication. The concepts of many great and good peoples' minds flow through us, and that singu-

14

lar and privileged experience is incomparable in its value.

However, the greatest benefit to becoming a highly skilled interpreter is the interaction we have with the Deaf community. Few people in the hearing world ever notice this vibrant, powerful, and loving culture that exists around them every day. It is a culture whose values and beliefs are sorely needed in today's world and whose communication is straightforward and honest.

We as interpreters must never forget the honor and privilege we have in being placed in a position of trust by our Deaf clients and their hearing counterparts with whom they interact. This trust is one of the greatest gifts that can be extended to us, and one which we should always hold as a torch to guide our way as we master our skills and develop our profession. So whether you are just beginning your journey, or have been on this path for many years, I hope the concepts within this work have helped you on your way, and that our paths cross down the road.